FINDING OUR WAY B

PRAYING OUR WAY FORWARD

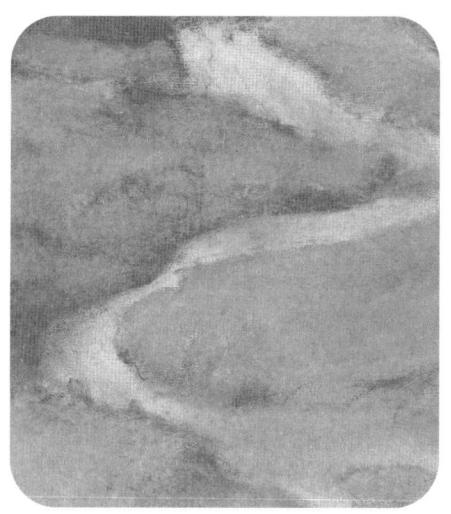

FINDING OUR WAY BACK
PRAYING OUR WAY FORWARD

Prayer moments
for Lent, Holy Week,
Advent, Christmas
and beyond

Rebeka Maples

wild goose
publications

www.ionabooks.com

Copyright © 2023 Rebeka Maples

First published 2023 by
Wild Goose Publications
Suite 9, Fairfield
1048 Govan Road, Glasgow G51 4XS, Scotland
the publishing division of the Iona Community.
Scottish Charity No. SC003794. Limited Company Reg. No. SC096243.

ISBN 978-1-80432-283-3

Cover illustration from 'Pathway in a Field', painting by Edgar Degas

All rights reserved. Apart from the circumstances described below relating to non-commercial use, no part of this publication may be reproduced in any form or by any means, including photocopying or any information storage or retrieval system, without written permission from the publisher via PLSclear.com.

Non-commercial use: The material in this book may be used non-commercially for worship and group work without written permission from the publisher. If photocopies of sections are made, please make full acknowledgement of the source, and report usage to CLA or other copyright organisation.

Rebeka Maples has asserted her right in accordance with the Copyright, Designs and Patents Act, 1988, to be identified as the author of this work.

Overseas distribution
Australia: Willow Connection Pty Ltd, 1/13 Kell Mather Drive,
Lennox Head NSW 2478
New Zealand: Pleroma, Higginson Street, Otane 4170,
Central Hawkes Bay

Printed in the UK by Page Bros (Norwich) Ltd

Finding our way back, praying our way forward 5

CONTENTS

Introduction   9

PRAYER MOMENTS ON THE LENTEN JOURNEY:
CARNIVAL TO EASTER SUNDAY AND BEYOND   13

First week Of Lent

Sunday before Ash Wednesday (Beginning of Carnival)   15
Monday before Ash Wednesday   17
Shrove Tuesday   19
Ash Wednesday   20
Thursday, first week of Lent   22
Friday, first week of Lent   23
Saturday, first week of Lent   24

Second week of Lent

Sunday, second week of Lent   27
Monday, second week of Lent   28
Tuesday, second week of Lent   29
Wednesday, second week of Lent   31
Thursday, second week of Lent   32
Friday, second week of Lent   33
Saturday, second week of Lent   34

Third week of Lent

Sunday, third week of Lent   37
Monday, third week of Lent   38
Tuesday, third week of Lent   39
Wednesday, third week of Lent   41
Thursday, third week of Lent   42
Friday, third week of Lent   44
Saturday, third week of Lent   45

Fourth week of Lent

Sunday, fourth week of Lent   48
Monday, fourth week of Lent   49
Tuesday, fourth week of Lent   51
Wednesday, fourth week of Lent   52
Thursday, fourth week of Lent   54
Friday, fourth week of Lent   55
Saturday, fourth week of Lent   56

Fifth week of Lent

Sunday, fifth week of Lent   59
Monday, fifth week of Lent   60
Tuesday, fifth week of Lent   62
Wednesday, fifth week of Lent   63
Thursday, fifth week of Lent   64
Friday, fifth week of Lent   66
Saturday, fifth week of Lent   68

Sixth week of Lent

Sunday, sixth week of Lent   71
Monday, sixth week of Lent   72
Tuesday, sixth week of Lent   74
Wednesday, sixth week of Lent   75
Thursday, sixth week of Lent   77
Friday, sixth week of Lent   78
Saturday, sixth week of Lent   80

Holy Week

Palm/Passion Sunday   83
Monday in Holy Week   85
Tuesday in Holy Week   87
Wednesday in Holy Week   88

Holy Thursday   90
Good Friday   92
Holy Saturday   94
Easter Sunday   96

The Easter season
Second Sunday of Easter   99
The day of Pentecost   100

PRAYER MOMENTS IN OUR ADVENT WAITING: CHRIST THE KING SUNDAY TO CHRISTMAS AND BEYOND   103

Introduction   104
Christ the King Sunday   106

First week of Advent
Sunday, first week in Advent   109
Monday, first week in Advent   110
Tuesday, first week in Advent   111
Wednesday, first week in Advent   112
Thursday, first week in Advent   114
Friday, first week in Advent   116
Saturday, first week in Advent   117

Second week of Advent
Sunday, second week in Advent   120
Monday, second week in Advent   121
Tuesday, second week in Advent   123
Wednesday, second week in Advent   124
Thursday, second week in Advent   125
Friday, second week in Advent   126
Saturday, second week in Advent   128

Third week of Advent

Sunday, third week in Advent   131
Monday, third week in Advent   132
Tuesday, third week in Advent   133
Wednesday, third week in Advent   134
Thursday, third week in Advent   135
Friday, third week in Advent   136
Saturday, third week in Advent   137

Fourth week of Advent

Sunday, fourth week in Advent   140
Monday, fourth week in Advent   141
Tuesday, fourth week in Advent   142
Wednesday, fourth week in Advent   143
Thursday, fourth week in Advent   145
Christmas Eve   146
Christmas Day   147

After Christmas Day

First Sunday after Christmas Day   150
Epiphany of the Lord   151
Baptism of the Lord   153
Presentation of the Lord/Candlemas   154

Praying our way forward   156
Sources and acknowledgements   159

INTRODUCTION

The prayers in this book are from my devotions in different places, at different times of the year, through the Covid pandemic and other struggles, and are an offering to our collective prayers for the world and each other as we find our way back from lockdowns and setbacks and pray our way forward to a new normal in the holy seasons of our lives.

In my morning devotions during the coronavirus pandemic, I realised how much I had been focusing on myself. It was probably natural; after all it was a time of staying home and social distancing; an opportunity to look inward and reflect on self-improvement and spiritual growth. The challenge was how to maintain a balanced sense of self and community while confined to one physical place.

I kept asking myself: when would things get back to normal? And kept returning to this verse from Micah:

> *He has told you, O mortal, what is good;*
> *and what does the Lord require of you*
> *but to do justice, and to love kindness,*
> *and to walk humbly with your God? (Mic 6:8, NRSV)*

After reading those words, it occurred to me that getting 'back to normal' is not about getting back to the way things were; it is about getting back to what God calls me to do – and that is to do justice, to love kindness, and to walk humbly with God. God leads us into the future and walks with us, no matter where that leads. Walking through these holy seasons reminds me that God's love is not back there, but where I am, in 'normal' and 'in-between' times.

These readings are for daily devotion during Lent/Holy Week, Advent/Christmas, and beyond. The liturgical seasons are useful markers in the Christian year. They guide our prayers and help us through all that is going on in our lives. As we journey through the holy seasons we make the connection between incarnation and resurrection, birth and redemptive passion.

Each day in the book begins with a short passage from scripture (using readings from the Revised Common Lectionary) and is followed by a poem for reflection, a 'prayer moment' with a suggestion for meditation or action, and a short prayer for you to continue with your own prayer.

My hope is that you will find a part of your story in the ancient text, ask questions of the Mystery of God, sink into the space of prayer and meditation and feel new life being breathed into you. The Breath of Life weaves the tattered strands of our lives together; torn pieces are reframed into a tapestry of completeness. Nothing is lost and all is made whole.

My prayer is that you emerge from these sacred moments and return to the world with a sense of hope, knowing the Mystery of the unknowable is, indeed, the Source of all that gives new life.

Waiting for the light

The year is filled with light from holy seasons.
We move through each season
and bring our weary light-deprived souls with us,
as if there is no light, as if it only shines on Christmas and Easter,
on the righteous, the lucky, or the blessed,
and then leaves until next year.
But light is a part of life, a gift for everyone that never dies.
It surrounds us and breathes over us and through us all year.

It blinds us and blesses us.
Light finds a way, when there is no way.
Light is a lamp in the darkness and a beacon
through the storms that bombard us on the journey.

We are all bearers of Christmas and Easter light.
Always seeking more, we carry a spark of that which we seek within us,
an ember of something holy from the beginning of time.
And it is that light, that holiness,
that gives us hope and shines in and from us
throughout the year.
If we wait and listen long enough, we will find the light,
and hope will return.
Light finds a way, when there is no way.
The light that shines in the darkness never leaves.
We begin the journey
finding our way back, praying our way forward,
waiting for the light.

Rebeka Maples

PRAYER MOMENTS ON THE LENTEN JOURNEY:

Carnival to Easter Sunday and beyond

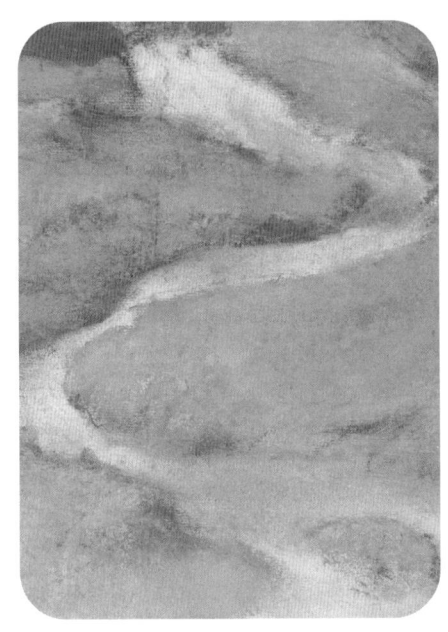

FIRST WEEK OF LENT

SUNDAY BEFORE ASH WEDNESDAY (Beginning of Carnival)

And all of us, with unveiled faces, seeing the glory of the Lord as though reflected in a mirror, are being transformed into the same image from one degree of glory to another; for this comes from the Lord, the Spirit.

2 Corinthians 3:18 (NRSV)

I wear the mask

I wear the mask in Ordinary Time
to hide my sin.
Yesterday, I wore the mask to keep
a vicious virus out.
Today, I wear the mask to hide my face
and celebrate in the revelry of Mardi Gras.
I'll laugh and drink and eat all I can
wearing shiny beads and having fun.

Today, I wear the mask.
Tomorrow, we begin the fast,
forty days of fleeing Satan's grasp.
We'll sing our final Alleluia
and bury it from sight,
until we sing it again in Easter's morning light.

Tonight, I wear the mask
and dance with God.
Tomorrow, I face the wilderness;
Ash Wednesday marks the way.
I'll hide behind this mask
and let it slip away,

not because the battle has been won,
it has only just begun.

Finally, all the masks must fall,
all the laughing and cheering must end,
so too the mockery and hate.
Then, we enter the Great Silence
and wait for life dying on a cross,
praying for the veil to be lifted.

Tonight, tomorrow,
this is the day the Lord has made,
let us rejoice and be glad in it. *(Ps 118:24, NRSV)*

Prayer moment

Many of the church's traditions have been lost or forgotten through the years. Few recognise, as preparation for Lent, the raucous celebrations of Mardi Gras or Carnival in the days before Ash Wednesday. In the revelry of the parades and parties of Carnival, the mask played a central role. At the end of the Carnival feasts, the masks came off and the last 'Alleluia' was sung; then written on a piece of paper and buried in a box. This was the sign that fasting would begin and 'Alleluia' would not be sung again until Easter morning. These traditions were reminders of Jesus' entrance into the desert for forty days. What reminders, signs, traditions do you have?

As you enter this season of Lent, prepare a 'prayer space'. Gather there items that are meaningful to you: a journal or notebook, pens, a candle, prayer beads, a holding cross or stones, music …

To begin, hold one of your pandemic facemasks and reflect on what that time has meant to you. Pray for frontline workers and victims of the coronavirus. Thank God for providing us with ways to protect ourselves. Looking at your mask, think of all the other types of masks you wear in the course of a day, a week, a year, a life. End your prayer time by thanking God for seeing behind all our many disguises.

Alleluia, God of feasts and fasts! Whether joy or grief, whether peace or pain, I pray that I will find my way back to you through this Lenten journey, knowing you are there behind every mask and in each step along the way …

MONDAY BEFORE ASH WEDNESDAY

All the skillful women spun with their hands, and brought what they had spun in blue and purple and crimson yarns and fine linen; all the women whose hearts moved them to use their skill spun the goats' hair.

Exodus 35:25–26 (NRSV)

> There in our worried selves we were
> surrounded by a virus seeking ever to destroy.
> Unable to avoid its trap
> we scrambled to unwind ourselves from each other,
> from a virus that came from another world,
> unknown to any of us before it was known to all of us.
> Now to find a better way, a clearer path to life and love.
>
> Lent, a time of fasting, depriving and denying.
> Woven through a pandemic, time of changing, moving away.
> Bound together in a greater Mystery, time of healing, turning back,

brought together in our distance, spinning our hearts in unity,
finding new ways to live in community.
Hope restored, lives renewed.

Prayer moment

The women spun yarn and wove their hearts together. As you prepare for the season of Lent, what one thing can you do this week with any feelings of being disconnected? Phone a friend, write them a note, pray for a stranger, read about other people's struggles, look for something (small or big) that connects you to the world?

God of quiet struggles and loud cries, hear my prayer this day for all that separates me from others and all that binds us together …

SHROVE TUESDAY

There is nothing better for mortals than to eat and drink, and find enjoyment in their toil. This also, I saw, is from the hand of God ...

Ecclesiastes 2:24 (NRSV)

Enjoy the good things

Now we enjoy the good things of life,
taking our fill of food and drink.
We crown ourselves with flowers of spring,
making merry before they wither.
God in heaven gives all of this,
our daily soup and bread to scoop.
Today we taste the sweetness of milk and honey
as we feast and eat whatever we want.
Casseroles and desserts with too much starch and lots of butter,
we won't worry about calorie count or fat content.
We'll overeat on pasta and rice,
before the fast that starts with ashes and ends in light.
Then we'll know the grace of heaven
falling in the morning dew,
showering the earth with enough for all.
But now we feast before the fast,
praying to be more like Christ,
waiting until we dine again in Easter's light.

Prayer moment

Make a batch of pancakes for family and friends. As you eat and prepare for the Lenten journey, share ideas of an intentional act you could 'take on' (supporting a food pantry?) or 'give up' (wasting food?) as part of your Lenten 'fast'. Write about this in your journal and think about how this action will help to remind you of God's love throughout the forty days of Lent.

God of Shrovetide, come and help us enjoy the good things of life, give us this day our daily bread, and feed us on your Holy Word as we travel together down the Lenten road …

ASH WEDNESDAY

*Yet even now, says the Lord,
return to me with all your heart,
with fasting, with weeping, and with mourning;
rend your hearts and not your clothing …*

Joel 2:12–13a

Ashes, ashes, we all fall down

'Ashes, ashes, we all fall down' is a song for giggling children.
'Remember you are dust, and to dust you shall return'
is said on Ash Wednesday,
not to remember that you will die, but that you will live.

'Earth to earth, ashes to ashes, dust to dust' is said at funerals
for assurance in the hope of resurrection.

Our ashes are a sign of love and hope, dying and rising,
of grace etched on our foreheads and written in our hearts.
'Return to me,' says the Lord, 'and I will return to you.'

The Lenten fast is a reminder
of letting go or taking on.
God forgives and God's love never leaves.
From birth to death and beyond
God is with us.

Prayer moment

If you are able, attend an Ash Wednesday service, or remember the mark of ashes in prayer: not as a sign of gloom and doom but of new life to come. Place a bowl of sand or soil in your house where you can see and touch the sand/soil each day during Lent, remembering the dry places in your life that you want God to touch, and holding on to the promise that nothing will keep God's light from you.

God of desert places, pray with me now and throughout these forty days, so that when Easter finally comes I will be filled anew with joy for life and love for you …

THURSDAY, FIRST WEEK OF LENT

... the earth was a formless void and darkness covered the face of the deep, while a wind from God swept over the face of the waters.

Genesis 1:2 (NRSV)

> **Ruach: Spirit, wind, breath**
>
> Ruach is a Hebrew word for Spirit, wind and breath.
> In the beginning, the Spirit of God
> swept over the waters and breathed new life into creation.
> The wind of God blows.
> The Spirit brings us closer to God, urging us into prayer.
> Listen to the wind.
> Pray with or without the words. Breathe.
> Feel the presence of the breath of God breathing over you,
> surrounding you.

Prayer moment

Open a window or go outside and feel the wind or breezes blowing on your face. Take a deep breath and just be in the moment. Think of the times that Jesus must have felt the wind or breezes blowing on his face during his time in the wilderness, while he longed for the breath of God.

Gentle breath of Ruach, breathe over me, let my words fall away so I am prepared to listen in this holy season ...

FRIDAY, FIRST WEEK OF LENT

*I call upon you, for you will answer me, O God;
incline your ear to me, hear my words.*

Psalm 17:6 (NRSV)

Sacred space (On the holy island of Iona)

Praying in this place,
watching water flowing
waves crashing onto shore
surely something holy is here.

Celestial sky
morning light
green hills with sheep peering through the mist,
ancient ruins offering sacred space.

The holiness of memory draws me here
to stay and meet the blessings of creation,
to be held in the moment,
to know the sacredness of place.

Can such a time be found?
Can such a place have been?
Turn around and step into the space
where heaven and earth are one.

Prayer moment

The scripture holds stories of sacred moments of God appearing in different places. What are some sacred spaces for you? Recall times when you felt God's Spirit filling you with awe and wonder, in quiet peaceful places, on bustling city streets. Think of how both can be 'thin' places where heaven and earth meet. Return to these memories during the day, and at other times in your Lenten journey.

Creator of sacred space, I am praying to meet you again, to find you in the holiness of your story and of each place that welcomes me …

SATURDAY, FIRST WEEK OF LENT

The spirit of the Lord is upon me,
  because the Lord has anointed me;
he has sent me to bring good news to the oppressed,
  to bind up the brokenhearted,
to proclaim liberty to the captives,
  and release to the prisoners …

Isaiah 61:1 (NRSV)

In the rubble of your life

Look for your voice in the rubble of your life.
Let it rise from the ashes of dreams once glowing.

In the embers of the past,
a spark of hope will rise

and the song that was never sung
will echo from the depths of you
calling forth your life,
not to live the past
but to embrace the future
and live the life
that is waiting still for you.

Prayer moment

Think of a time when you needed to hear 'good news'. What was it and where did it come from? From someone expected? From someone unexpected? Thank God for sending you hope when you needed it most. Who might you contact during Lent to offer and share a word of hope?

Restorer of hope, hear the cries of all who are caught in webs of abuse and violence. May our Lenten prayers be prayers of freeing us from the hurtful cycles of our past ...

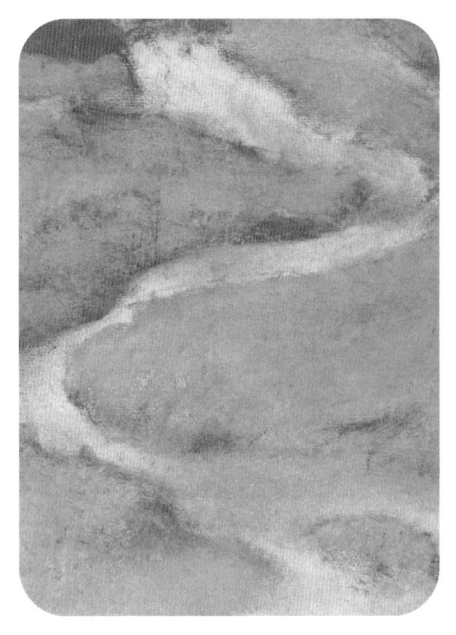

SECOND WEEK OF LENT

SUNDAY, SECOND WEEK OF LENT

Jesus, full of the Holy Spirit, returned from the Jordan and was led by the Spirit in the wilderness ...

Luke 4:1 (NRSV)

In this deserted place

Dwells the soul in this deserted place, lost and alone,
searching for love, for hope, for life,
dark and alone, as night without stars,
no light, no one, no thing.

Dwells the soul alone, in this deserted place,
aching for warmth, longing for love, wanting life again,
dark night of the soul, with no other soul around,
weakened by emptiness, cursed by memories
echoing through time.

The soul, wandering through shadows,
through silhouettes that glimmer in some hidden light,
lost and alone without the soul's desire,
waiting for its moment of awakening.

Prayer moment

Think of a time when you felt deserted, lost and alone. Did you come to feel God's presence at that time? How can we be present to each other in our 'dark night of the soul' in these Lenten days?

God of the wilderness, stumbling over possibilities I search for answers and wonder why I have sunk so low. Send your Spirit to lead me out of this wilderness and into the light of Easter ...

MONDAY, SECOND WEEK OF LENT

… where for forty days he was tempted by the devil. He ate nothing at all during those days, and when they were over, he was famished.

Luke 4:2 (NRSV)

Facing this deserted place

Dwells the soul in this deserted place,
gently moving, comes a breeze,
gently falling, drops of rain,
silently, unknowing, stars appear.

Dwells the soul in this deserted place,
slowly moving through this timeless void,
light casts shadows on the wall,
longing for life to awaken.

Dwells the soul in this deserted place,
moved by winds from a hidden Source,
night turns into day, day into night.
The soul dwells in emptiness,
facing this deserted place.

Prayer moment

Depression comes to all of us: one moment we feel God's presence everywhere, and the next, God seems nowhere, and we feel nothing, only loss, and our spirit sinks into feelings of sadness and despair. What helps you, or what might you do, when you have these feelings? Think of someone who is struggling and send them a note of encouragement during this week of Lent.

I know, God, you are a God of all places, dry and empty, joyful and serene, so I pray this simple prayer during my Lenten journey: find me and lift me from the abyss that I seem to be falling into …

TUESDAY, SECOND WEEK OF LENT

And he dreamed that there was a ladder set up on the earth, the top of it reaching to heaven; and the angels of God were ascending and descending on it.

Genesis 28:12 (NRSV)

White helmets

White Helmets of light,
roaming through rubble
clawing and scraping
looking for hope
finding breath inside of death.

White Helmets of light,
looking for life buried below
scratching the surface
digging in concrete
revealing the hope that is still there.

White Helmets of light, angels of God,
bringing songs from heaven
finding light in the fires of hell
rescuing the spark that bombs cannot kill
reclaiming hope in remnants of death.

White Helmets of light,
perfecting the good
piecing together the pieces of love
writing hope on the lips of the dying
lifting the curtain before it closes.

White Helmets of light,
constructors of peace
preservers of hope,
you are the answer
the world cannot find.

Prayer moment

'The White Helmets' is a group of civil defence volunteers in Syria (see www.whitehelmets.org and *The White Helmets* on YouTube, from Netflix). In spite of danger to themselves, these frontline responders search through the bombed-out wreckage of Syria's civil war for any sign of life. Thousands of people have been saved by them. The 'White Helmets' are ordinary citizens doing extraordinary things, restoring hope.

Give thanks for these everyday heroes, for their work and for being a shining light for the rest of humanity. Pray for frontline responders around the world and in your community.

God of all hope, send blessings on the White Helmet volunteers in Syria and on all other frontline responders. Open my eyes to the pain of others that I may be a part of the earth's healing, not its destruction …

WEDNESDAY, SECOND WEEK OF LENT

So we do not lose heart. Even though our outer nature is wasting away, our inner nature is being renewed day by day.

2 Corinthians 4:16 (NRSV)

Spring's eternal light

Nature holds the terrestrial gift,
and pleads forgiveness for our reckless waste and
thoughtless greed;
on rolling hills with daffodils, amber fields and mountain streams,
our deeds follow us, and now we pray our pardon will be swift.

We hold the lamp in the starless night
piercing holes in heaven's dome;
step by step we move, closer to the Source
of life and love, and spring's eternal light.

Prayer moment

Go outside and look for signs of spring: buds on trees, flowers poking through snow and frost, longer days of light thawing the winter inside you.

Light Maker, through these cold and barren Lenten nights, I long to see the rising light of spring and know your love is coming …

THURSDAY, SECOND WEEK OF LENT

I will set my bow in the clouds, and it shall be a sign of the covenant between me and the earth.

Genesis 9:13 (NRSV)

Rainbow of blessings (After the rain on the Isle of Iona)

Rainbows of light appear in the sky –
and I wonder, why?
One when we walked on the shore
   saying, where you are is blessed.
Another when we turned around
there, where we had been –
a beautiful arc of colour
   saying, where you have been is blessed.
Then looking through the window pane,
another reached across the sea
hovering brilliantly,
   saying, where you are going is blessed.
A rainbow of blessings –
gives meaning to life
past, present, future,
   saying: who you are is blessed.

Prayer moment

I saw these rainbows while walking with a friend across Iona on a rainy day. What and who are some of the gifts of love that God has brought into your life? Hold them in your prayer and feel their presence. Think of the beauty of rainbows and what meaning they may provide for you during the long days of Lent.

God of rainbow blessings, during these forty days, may I see and receive the gifts of love that you present to me ...

FRIDAY, SECOND WEEK OF LENT

He answered, 'You shall love the Lord your God with all your heart, and with all your soul, and with all your strength, and with all your mind; and your neighbour as yourself.'

Luke 10:27 (NRSV)

Is that love?

Love God and love your neighbour as yourself –
easy to say, not so easy to do.
What is love?
Christians often say they love God,
while condemning those who look or live differently than they do.
Is that love?
Even violence hides behind the guise of love.
A woman says she loves a man even though he abuses her.
Is that love?
Many people look in the mirror and hate what they see,
even though each of us reflects the image of God.
Is that love?

Divine love never stops seeking ways to bless us, ways to love us,
with morning light and peace at night.
Love what God loves –
that is love!

Prayer moment

During today's Lenten prayer, think of someone in your life you could be kinder to. Hold that person in prayer. And how might you be kinder to yourself? Touch the sand/soil in your Lenten bowl and pray for God's love to guide you through each day of Lent.

O Heart of love, help me to let go of the world's understanding of love; awaken the seed of love that you have planted in my heart, that Easter's morning light may shine through me even in desert times …

SATURDAY, SECOND WEEK OF LENT

They said to each other, 'Were not our hearts burning within us while he was talking to us on the road, while he was opening the scriptures to us?'

Luke 24:32 (NRSV)

O moon of hallowed dreams

In the sounds of evening slowly creeping into night,
I sit in silent expectation, waiting.

Will the moon shine full with all its glory,
or retreat behind invading clouds?

What could a full moon offer, if it offered anything:
a majestic spectacle of colour and dazzling light?

Sitting in repose with sounds of evening descending into night,
slowly life transforms in the changing of the light.

Trees that stood in blazing leaf-dom
evolve into creatures stalking through the night.

O moon of hallowed dreams,
will you come in that orange glow rising from the ground?

Will your silhouette appear and trace
the scars emblazoned on your soul?

In the mystical hue of the darkening sky
a faint halo lingers then slowly disappears.

The moon, full of mystery, would not come my way tonight,
alas, another time.

What was in this place of rising moons and setting suns
and I did not know?

Prayer moment

It was after Easter and the disciples were walking on the road to Emmaus with Jesus right there next to them. How could they have missed him? Sometimes we miss what is right in front of us because we are expecting things to look or be a certain way or because we are preoccupied. During your Lenten meditation, think of a time when you might have missed Jesus right there by your side.

God of mystery, why it is that I miss your presence? Come and open my eyes during my Lenten prayers that I may see you with new understanding …

THIRD WEEK OF LENT

SUNDAY, THIRD WEEK OF LENT

I believe that I shall see the goodness of the Lord
  in the land of the living.
Wait for the Lord;
  be strong, and let your heart take courage;
  wait for the Lord!

Psalm 27:13–14 (NRSV)

This wilderness

Turn my eyes from pain and despair
to what is good and full of life.
Take me out of this wilderness and prepare me
for the journey that leads to life.

This wilderness is full of chaos.
This wilderness is out of control.
This wilderness is like a virus wilder than the desert,
wilder than the tyranny of greed and power.

This wilderness is a way out, full of prayer and fasting,
full of waiting for another way.
Step by step, day by day,
nothing heroic, nothing amazing, only waiting.
Look! There is a table in this wilderness
poured out with living water, set with bread from heaven.

Prayer moment

What is worrying you most during this season of Lent? What will give you courage and a sense of hope? Think of one small act of kindness that you can offer to yourself today, and to someone else.

Heart of mercy, the days are quickly passing and I seem to be standing still, going nowhere. Fill me with courage enough to make even small changes that give my life a sense of purpose and wholeness, as I travel this ancient desert road in this wilderness time …

MONDAY, THIRD WEEK OF LENT

He said to them, 'Go and tell that fox for me, "Listen, I am casting out demons and performing cures today and tomorrow, and on the third day I finish my work … "'

Luke 13:32

Beneath the words

Beneath the words,
where silence finds a voice
in the noise of the world,
listen to what you do not hear
and you will hear a life not lived,
you will hear a story not told.

Let Spirit be
and find its home.
Keep on searching

beneath the words
until
you live again.

Prayer moment

Listening is a difficult task, a sacred art. How often do you find your mind wandering when someone is talking to you, or you interrupting them? For today's Lenten act of kindness, practise listening: do not let yourself interrupt, and do not try to 'fix' the other person. Just practise listening. Know that God is listening with you.

Silent Listener, send your Spirit into my life that I may be renewed in your love. I am tired of dreaming of ways to follow you; come and come quickly, as I listen for you in my Lenten praying …

TUESDAY, THIRD WEEK OF LENT

No testing has overtaken you that is not common to everyone. God is faithful, and he will not let you be tested beyond your strength, but with the testing he will also provide the way out so that you may be able to endure it.

1 Corinthians 10:13 (NRSV)

The labyrinth

Following the way of the ancient prayer labyrinth,
I enter with a question and slowly walk the path
to the centre and out again,
praying along the way, searching for answers.

There are no dead ends or wrong turns in the labyrinth,
only one way in, one way out,
through all the twists and turns
of my life.
Some roads I took were not the best,
I did not follow the higher one,
but wandered through a maze of blind alleyways
until I came to where I am today,
still praying and stumbling,
but finding answers another way.

Prayer moment

If possible, find an indoor or outdoor labyrinth and make plans to walk the sacred journey sometime during Lent. Or print a labyrinth pattern (see www.labyrinthsociety.org) which you can trace with your finger or a pencil. Do your walking or tracing slowly, prayerfully. Begin with a prayer or question for God, and continue focusing on the path; when your mind wanders, return to the path, not trying to find answers. When you finish, say a prayer of thanks for God's prayerful presence, and ask God to continue to be with you on your journey through Lent. You may want to journal about this experience.

Thanks to the Holy One for signposts to higher roads and for the courage to follow them on my journey ...

WEDNESDAY, THIRD WEEK OF LENT

He put before them another parable: 'The kingdom of heaven is like a mustard seed that someone took and sowed in his field …'

Matthew 13:31 (NRSV)

Through frozen ground

The seed lies dormant in frozen ground,
waiting for spring rains to filter through with hope,
waiting for the light,
waiting for warm winds and summer sun
to thaw the frigid earth.
Waiting,
lying dormant while other seeds begin to grow
and other soil is turned.
Still sleeping it waits as new seeds are scattered.
Waiting, always waiting,
as the rising sun and falling moon make their rounds.
Waiting,
the seed does not beg for growth,
only waits for new life to awaken.
Rains come and winds blow,
sun shines and the seed senses something stirring.
Filled with desire for what lies ahead,
waiting gives way to a new day,
touched by light
growing among other seeds
dormant no longer
new life comes
through frozen ground.

Prayer moment

Sit outside or in a quiet place and reflect on what Lent means to you. What words in this poem resonate with you? Describe what comes to your mind. What lessons in life have helped to spark seeds of new growth in you? Where do you see a new seed growing in someone else's life? What spiritual seeds might you plant during Lent?

O Spirit of heaven and earth, during this season of Lent, breathe your healing touch into the broken places in my life, revive my soul and restore the seed of hope so life may grow again ...

THURSDAY, THIRD WEEK OF LENT

For everything there is a season, and a time for every matter under heaven ...

Ecclesiastes 3:1 (NRSV)

Every season matters

Every choice, every season matters
in the course of a life.
Seasons come and seasons go,
autumn, winter, spring, summer,
each affects the other,
each part intertwined
in an inescapable web of mutuality.
One leads into the other,
one choice, one breath
one sunset, one breeze
affects all the others.

A quiet moment in the sun,
watching trees in their regal display,
chasing leaves as they fall,
gathering fruit in their season,
each one makes the next one matter.
In the autumn of my life,
every choice, every season matters.

Prayer moment

What's your favourite season of the year? What are some things you like most about that season? Close your eyes and think about a time when you felt close to God: where were you? What season was it? Now write your thoughts and say a prayer of thanks for all the seasons of your life and the changes God will bring to you in this Lenten season.

Giver of all time, as I enter this day may I become aware of the season I am in; may I learn to not indulge my worries, to not take myself so seriously, and to give thanks for the gift of life ...

FRIDAY, THIRD WEEK OF LENT

O God, you are my God, I seek you,
  my soul thirsts for you;
my flesh faints for you,
  as in a dry and weary land where there is no water.

Psalm 63:1 (NRSV)

Praying and fasting

Praying and fasting
my soul grows weary, waiting
for the One who fasted forty days in the wilderness.
Thirst guides me
and my heart takes courage,
yearning for the One who will lead me through
these dry and empty days.
The drama of the journey to the cross,
the feelings of betrayal and abandonment
make the story live in me
and lead me deeper into its mystery,
with the image of the Holy One praying
and fasting with me, calling me closer,
never giving up on me.

Prayer moment

Set a glass or bowl of water in front of you. Read the scripture verse again slowly. What images come to mind? What thoughts? Touch the water and put a few drops on your forehead or hand, then close your eyes and sit quietly, thinking of Jesus and his thirst in desert places and on the cross.

Think of those who need clean, safe water. Find an article about or images of a water conservation project, then pray for the people and places named or shown there. What habits might you change during Lent to become more aware of the precious gift of water?

I lift my prayers to you, Heart of all hearts. In this time and with your love, may I be aware of the gift of water and the ways you are guiding me through wilderness places …

SATURDAY, THIRD WEEK OF LENT

So I have looked upon you in the sanctuary,
 beholding your power and glory.

Psalm 63:2 (NRSV)

The heart of creation

(Inspired by Vasquez Rocks Natural Area in southern California)

Layers of rock and sand pressed into the earth,
millions of years
of volcanoes, earthquakes, glaciers, fire and rain,
desert land now exposing monuments of memory.
Jutting from the earth, piercing the sky,
a displacement of nature,
creation in formation,
barren land with beauty hidden in sight.
Low valley of green fed by an underground stream,
plants flowering, stems holding buds and fragrant leaves,

shades of red and orange painted on walls of layered rock.
Steep cliffs and rolling hills in heat of sun,
layers of geology,
a wonder in archaeology.
Mystery of change carries memory
from the beginning,
nothing holds it in place
but the heart of creation.

Prayer moment

If possible, visit a geological formation and spend some time there in meditation or journaling. Or search through a travel or nature book and find an image that attracts you. Sit quietly with the picture and imagine yourself there. What feelings do you experience? What memories of places you've visited come to your mind? For today's Lenten prayer, spend time thanking God for the beauty and wonder of creation.

Source of all creation, there is so much in the world to comprehend: slow me down during this season of Lent so I may see and hear your presence in the beauty of nature that surrounds me …

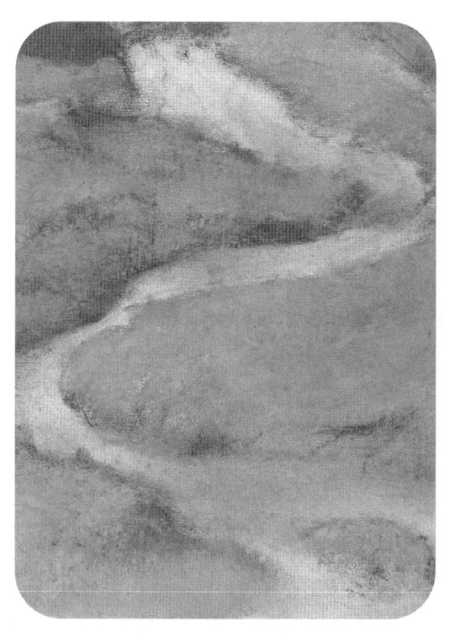

FOURTH WEEK OF LENT

SUNDAY, FOURTH WEEK OF LENT

Seek the Lord while he may be found,
  call upon him while he is near ...

Isaiah 55:6

For all the souls

For all the souls
who labour still while we rest:
may their unending gift
serve to lead others;
may the hope that held them on the frontlines
be a guiding light for us
who wait for a new day;
and may we keep believing
in the good that lingers near,
always waiting, always calling
until we too
from our labours rest.

For all the souls who know:
one suffering affects all,
One great suffering saved us all,
always near, always asking
to carry a part of that suffering, to heal a portion of it.
All our labour, all our rest is with the One
who was, who is, and always will be near.

Prayer moment

As part of your Lenten 'fast', find stories and names of frontline workers and pray for their work. You might write a note of thanks and send it to their workplace, or keep it as a prayer. Our prayers are part of our healing.

God of all that is, hear our prayers for those who are suffering and for those who help to relieve suffering. Help us to believe that you are with us and that we are able to make a difference together, with you wherever we are …

MONDAY, FOURTH WEEK OF LENT

Heaven and earth will pass away, but my words will not pass away.

Mark 13:31 (NRSV)

One place and another

In one place
soothing sounds of morning breeze,
birds chirping in the trees
train rumbling on the track.

In another
terrifying sounds of bombs exploding,
children screaming in the streets
voices moaning from the blast.

One place and another,
none of this is fair,

yet love is everywhere
bringing words of hope in life and death.
Joy in the morning
fear at night,
all of this will pass
in the coming light.

Prayer moment

With so much tragedy in the world, it is easy to lose hope and somehow think that God is causing war and suffering, but God does not destroy what God created. God suffers with those who suffer and cries with those who cry. God prays for us and needs us to pray. Be intentional during your Lenten prayers, lifting up places and people who are suffering, and being Christ's hands in the world.

Divine Word that does not leave, fill me with hope and the joy of your love, even when the chaos of life surrounds me …

TUESDAY, FOURTH WEEK OF LENT

But since we belong to the day, let us be sober, and put on the breastplate of faith and love, and for a helmet the hope of salvation.

1 Thessalonians 5:8 (NRSV)

Weapons of power

Carry them with you wherever you go –
love and understanding are power,
the best weapons of war and peace.

Carry them with you and use them whenever you can –
love and understanding will set you and the world free,
justice will reign and hope will rise.
Anger and hate cannot last,
rich and poor, black and white, all are connected
in the same thread of destiny.

Carry them with you –
breastplates of love and helmets of understanding.
Your words are power,
your actions are answers to someone's prayer.
Truth is not an edgeless sword,
it pierces hate and carves out justice.
Love with compassion, seek understanding,
use words only when necessary.

Carry your power and use it wherever you are –
love and understanding will never run out.

Unleash them, share them, and don't hold back,
no evil can stop what you hold in your heart.
Nothing can silence
love and understanding
when they thunder through history
transforming the world
unfettered and free.

Prayer moment

How could your actions be the answer to someone's prayer during Lent? Who in your family, church or community needs support? Perhaps someone needs to hear a kind word, or needs a lift to a doctor appointment. Organise a few people to respond to some of your community's needs, or find a charity near you that provides opportunities to volunteer.

Source of all understanding, fill me with hope that I may wear the strength of your love to encourage myself and others throughout these Lenten days …

WEDNESDAY, FOURTH WEEK OF LENT

When I look at your heavens, the work of your fingers,
  the moon and the stars that you have established;
what are human beings that you are mindful of them,
  mortals that you care for them?

Psalm 8:3–4 (NRSV)

Watching stars

Look into the midnight sky,
watch the stars as they fall.

Count them one by one,
they are not dying after all.

They are coming to the earth,
a blessing from our birth.

We were not born to count the stars,
and watch them from afar.

We were born to follow stars,
and count them where we are.

It would only empty us,
if our counting were a curse.

For watching stars as they fall
is a gift that blesses all.

Prayer moment

During Jesus' forty days in the desert the skies would have been full of stars, and Jesus most likely sat and meditated on scripture and recited the Psalms, including this one. Sometime during Lent, try to go outside somewhere where you can see the stars. Sit for a while in your stargazing and meditate, thinking of Jesus and how he too experienced the wonder of God's creation.

Star Thrower, when the stars are falling and when they are hidden, I will find hope in the beauty of your creation …

THURSDAY, FOURTH WEEK OF LENT

Then the Lord said to him, 'Take off the sandals from your feet, for the place where you are standing is holy ground.'

Acts 7:33 (NRSV)

Bridges to holy ground

In thin places, in holy spaces,
sanctuaries and hillsides, gardens and cornfields,
on city streets or country lanes,
life is lived on holy ground.

Two disciples were walking on the road to Emmaus
with Jesus himself,
but they did not realise who he was until later *(Lk 24:32)*.

God had to speak to Moses through a burning bush in order
to get his attention,
because he did not know he was standing on holy ground *(Ex 3:5)*.

We too can step into holy space and stand on holy ground
unaware of the sacredness of the moment until later.

Life is full of holy moments, bridges to holy ground,
where beauty or memory of a place takes your breath away.
When this happens take your sandals off
and walk around:
the place where you are standing is holy ground.

Prayer moment

Where have you found yourself on holy ground? Think back to a time when you felt God's presence and imagine yourself there. Recall the details of the environment and remember the feelings you had. Thank God for being so close that you felt God's presence, and say a blessing for that place.

Holy One, when I stumble into your presence during Lent, in scripture or in nature, let this be a sign for me to stop and listen, to look further into your Word and reflect or walk around in the space where I am …

FRIDAY, FOURTH WEEK OF LENT

Then Mary said, 'Here am I, the servant of the Lord; let it be with me according to your word.' Then the angel departed from her.

Luke 1:38 (NRSV)

Awake now

Awake now,
you sleeping daughters,
for your beloved comes.
Greet her with your choicest fruits,
receive her, and be drunk with love.
Where has your beloved gone?

Awake now,
she comes through your wilderness.

Be guided by her love,
set her seal upon your heart
and listen for her voice,
for she is calling you.

Make haste for love is strong as death,
and many waters cannot quench the raging flame
burning deep inside of you
and moving in your soul.
Awake now, for your beloved comes.

Prayer moment

What does the image of Mary mean to you? What characteristics from the stories of Mary resonate with you? What women in your life (or in history) do you associate with her? Name those women in your Lenten prayer and carry their names with you throughout the day as encouragement. Thank God for women of faith and spirit.

Lover of my soul, here am I, and I long to know your love; awaken the passion that you have planted in my soul, even as you did with your servant Mary …

SATURDAY, FOURTH WEEK OF LENT

So I will display my greatness and my holiness and make myself known in the eyes of many nations. Then they shall know that I am the Lord.

Ezekiel 38:23 (NRSV)

Chasing after holiness

Chasing after holiness,
longing for the light
sun sending flares of colour through the evening sky
red wall of fire falling in the trees
orange ball of brightness sitting on the edge.

Chasing after holiness
yearning for the light
hoping for a glimpse, to fill the emptiness
seeking higher ground, to get a better view.

Chasing after holiness
is futile in the end
for holiness will find you
and meet you where you are.

Prayer moment

This poem makes me laugh because I wrote it when I was on a retreat, anxious to see a beautiful sunset. The problem was, I kept moving from one spot to another to get the best view, and only saw the very end of the red sky fading behind the trees. What is so gratifying about a sunset? Where have you seen a beautiful sunset that filled you with awe? If possible, plan to watch the sunset sometime during Lent. Spend time afterwards praying and writing about what you saw and felt.

Holy One, slow me down during this Lenten time, so I may see you in what is around me; give me vision to be in the moment and see beyond what my eyes can see ...

FIFTH WEEK OF LENT

SUNDAY, FIFTH WEEK OF LENT

... but those who wait for the Lord shall renew their strength,
  they shall mount up with wings like eagles,
they shall run and not be weary,
  they shall walk and not faint.

Isaiah 40:31 (NRSV)

The heron's flight

What lifts the heron through the air?
A song without a word, a flight that has no care.
Outstretched wings lifting high,
soaring over rows of green and gold,
then gliding as though driven by a hidden source.

All of nature stops in awe to see the heron in its flight.
If I'm close enough and still enough,
I hear the slow and steady flapping of its wings.
Should I cry or should I sing at the joy of nature on the wing?
Someone of a holier time would fall on bended knee before
this holy thing.

Cry or sing anything you please
but pray, with any word or none. Pray
for the beauty of the heron taking flight,
to kiss the saints of heaven and catch the sun's early light.
I walk along the creek early in the morning –
and suddenly the world is awakened in my sight.

Prayer moment

On my early-morning walks when I lived near a farmer's cornfield, I often saw a lone heron taking flight from a creek as I approached. Those morning walks were a time of prayer when I would stop to journal or just listen to the sounds of nature before I began my day. If you are able, choose a morning during Lent to walk or sit in nature and pray, not necessarily saying words the whole time, not planning your day, but emptying your mind to just 'be' in the moment.

Holy of holies, I see your beauty in all creation and my heart wants to sing with joy. Help me be present to you during Lent that I may pray all ways ...

MONDAY, FIFTH WEEK OF LENT

'This is my commandment, that you love one another as I have loved you. No one has greater love than this, to lay down one's life for one's friends ...'

John 15:12–13 (NRSV)

When the light goes out

When friendship dies
and the light goes out,
the memory place cries with an aching emptiness
trying to erase what cannot be erased.

When friendship dies,
the grief and tears
speak to the mourning place.

Light once seen slowly disappears,
but the memories linger.

When friendship dies,
shock-waves are felt deep in the spirit place
and the soul wanders halls of the past
looking for light to open a door.

When friendship dies
be in the silent place.
Be alone with sadness
and bow to the sharing place,
until a glimmer of light returns
to the friendship place.

Prayer moment

Have you lost a friend, through death or other reasons? How did you feel? How did you cope with the loss? Spend some quiet time thinking and praying about what that friendship meant to you. Thank God for the blessings of friends. As a Lenten discipline, make a list of some of your friends and send a 'thinking of you' card to one each day.

Friend of the lost and lonely, hear my prayers for friends who come into my life for a time and leave; may I honour the gift that friendship offers in its time ...

TUESDAY, FIFTH WEEK OF LENT

You shall not cheat one another, but you shall fear your God; for I am the Lord your God.

Leviticus 25:17 (NRSV)

> We use our gifts to encourage others:
> paint the summer sky
> and harvest autumn's bounty,
> shape sculptures out of winter crystals
> and sow kindness in spring blossoms.
>
> We use our gifts to dismantle greed:
> to spread peace across the nations,
> offer blessings for strength,
> create memories of love,
> tell stories of hope.
>
> These gifts are treasures
> hidden in our hearts,
> buried in our past,
> held in our hands,
> waiting for discovery, a holy jubilee.
> Praise God, from whom all blessings flow!

Prayer moment

Lectio Divina (Sacred Reading) is an ancient practice of reading scripture slowly and contemplatively. Read the whole lectionary passage for today (Leviticus 25:1–19), then read it again. Stop and reflect on verse 17. How does the word 'cheat' affect you? Write or meditate on your thoughts and memories. Now, in your own time, slowly turn your feelings over to God. Rest in and feel God's love moving through you and blessing you in your Lenten prayer.

Guardian of my days, my spirit longs for the warmth and light of your love, signs to carry me deeper into the mystery of your Word, ways to change the world one word at a time …

WEDNESDAY, FIFTH WEEK OF LENT

If I take the wings of the morning
  and settle at the farthest limits of the sea,
even there your hand shall lead me,
  and your right hand shall hold me fast.

Psalm 139:9–10 (NRSV)

Morning on the wing

It's a glorious thing
to see morning on the wing.
It opens up before your eyes
  and leaves you mesmerised.
Many things may block your way
  keeping you in yesterday.
So do not walk away
  or rush into the day,
when morning opens up for you
  and gives you everything.

Prayer moment

Reflect on where you saw God's beauty today. What shade of green were the trees? Were there clouds, or a clear sky? Think of small changes you can make so that you do not miss the beauty of nature. Even when you are busy or feeling downhearted, pause and look up, take a moment to 'see'.

O Wings of dawn, in the wonder of your love, hold me in these Lenten days and let me see your beauty wherever I am …

THURSDAY, FIFTH WEEK OF LENT

… so that they may know, from the rising of the sun
  and from the west, that there is no one besides me;
  I am the Lord, and there is no other.

Isaiah 45:6 (NRSV)

Sun has risen

Sun has risen,
day is stirring,
waves are rushing onto shore,
life is scrambling to be heard.
Creation awakens
making haste,
noise of countless panting breaths
running forward, falling back,
holding on for love of life.

Sun is setting, day is fading
in the ebbing,
night is bringing light to end
in the flowing.
Creation now prepares for rest,
dreams unlived escape in time,
shadows hide what could have been.
Memories gather into sleep
leaving out what should have been,
giving hope another day.

Prayer moment

Do you have a memory of a beautiful sunrise you once experienced? Where were you? Recall that time and journal about what you saw and felt. If possible, plan a time during Lent to wake up early and watch the sunrise. Spend time reflecting on the wonder of God's love.

God of rising suns, let me feel the warmth of your embrace, so when the sun is rising on Easter morning, I will know you are Lord and there is no other ...

FRIDAY, FIFTH WEEK OF LENT

Let the words of my mouth and the meditation of my heart
  be acceptable to you,
  O Lord, my rock and my redeemer.

Psalm 19:14 (NRSV)

Pray as you can

When all is said and all is done,
you must pray as you can,
not as someone says you should.

Pray when your heart yearns for more.
Pray for the grace, pray for the forgiveness,
pray for the guidance, pray for the world ...
and then, let the words go.

Pray with your ears and listen.
Pray with your heart not your head.
Pray with words or none,
pray and feel your breath,
pray and sink into the moment.

There is nothing else
but you and the One who prays in you.
So go ahead, pray as you can, not as you can't.

Prayer moment

What are some of the ways that you pray? Make a list, then look for prayer books that suggest different ways of praying. Try a different way every week (or every day) in Lent. It took me a long time to accept that silence was prayer, that God was there no matter how I prayed. Start your prayer with an intentional act, such as lighting a candle or bowing, not for God to know that you are praying but to centre yourself.

O my God, how can I pray? There are no words forming in me and this is very strange for me. Teach me, that I may pray …

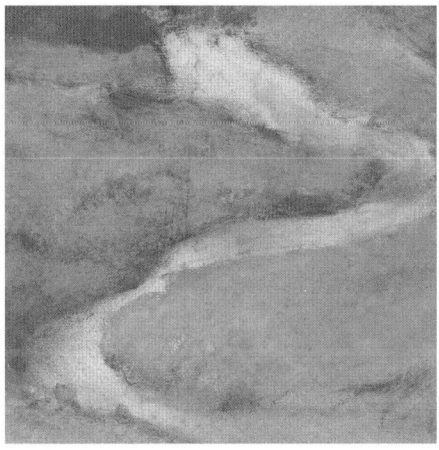

SATURDAY, FIFTH WEEK OF LENT

Peace I leave with you; my peace I give to you. I do not give to you as the world gives. Do not let your hearts be troubled, and do not let them be afraid.

John 14:27 (NRSV)

In the silent chapel

In the silent chapel of your heart,
hear the songs the angels sing,
pray the prayers that only you can pray.

Do not listen to other voices
tearing down and spreading fear;
give yourself other choices.

Go to that chapel in the corner of your heart
where hate has no hold;
surround yourself with peace and hope.

Wander through those holy places,
embrace the journey that leads to life,
leave fear and trouble in other spaces.

Prayer moment

If possible, plan a time during Lent to go to a chapel or another sacred place (it doesn't need to be a religious space) where you can sit still in the quiet. Read the Bible verse and poem, or a hymn from a songbook, as your prayer. Sit quietly, and when other things pop into your head gently set them aside.

Tell them that you know they are there and that you will tend to them later. For now, sit and practise being with God.

Source of peace, the trouble that surrounds me makes me afraid and I turn inward, seeing no way out. Give me strength to hold your words of peace in my heart, one day at a time, one prayer at a time …

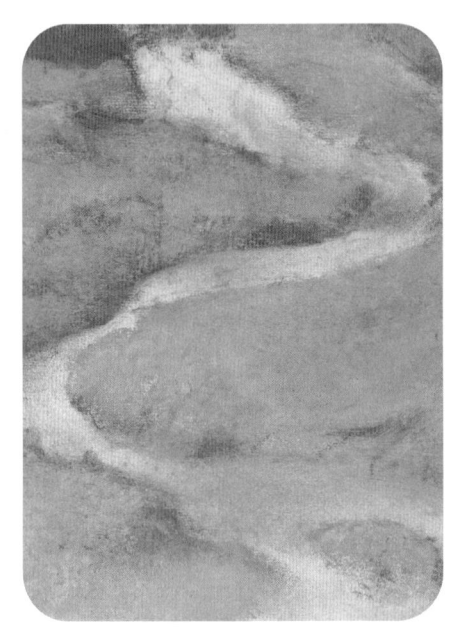

SIXTH WEEK OF LENT

SUNDAY, SIXTH WEEK OF LENT

I am about to do a new thing;
  now it springs forth, do you not perceive it?
I will make a way in the wilderness
  and rivers in the desert.

Isaiah 43:19 (NRSV)

A new way home

Spring calls to spring
for cleaning to begin,
to prepare a way for new life to come
and old to awake.

Spring brings the dead to life,
the seed to sprout.
All is made ready,
the earth is turned, the seed is sown.

Spring causes the heart to sing
and the soul to open its wings
for the flight to begin,
making a new way home.

Prayer moment

Gardening is a way of praying. If you have a garden plot, begin to till some of the earth, and gather a few seeds and plant them. You can also put some earth in a paper cup (even in a paper cup, God is there) and plant a few seeds there, or plant some seeds in your bowl of soil (see Ash Wednesday readings). Each day during Lent, water your seeds and wait for them to sprout. Do each step slowly and prayerfully. Think of the new life that will grow and thank God for the earth's life-giving gifts.

O Risen One, open me to your love in the emptiness of these Lenten days ...

MONDAY, SIXTH WEEK OF LENT

Beloved, let us love one another, because love is from God; everyone who loves is born of God and knows God.

1 John 4:7 (NRSV)

What love can do

Love what love can do
find what you can be
life is waiting here for you.

This is not the past
do not live there,
let the voices go
do not cling to what is gone.

This is not the future
you are not there yet,
let the worries be
do not live where you are not.

This is now
do not miss what love can do
no one else can live for you.
Live the life that you are in
you cannot live where you have been,
you cannot be where you are not.

Be in the time you are in.
No one can live for you
or be what you can be.
The time is now
the place is here.
Love and live what you can do
there is more waiting for you.

Prayer moment

Look back over your Lenten journey so far; read through your journal. What is the worry or challenge you focus on most? What are some of your hopes and dreams? In your reflection, consider what might help you to move forward and what you could let go of. Don't focus on trying to fix everything or on what is wrong, just examine the situation, then sit quietly and begin talking to God in your prayer or journal. Feel God's love moving through and around you. Know that God will help guide you in these Lenten days.

Loving God, I don't always understand love or you, yet I want to know love and I want to know you; find me and show me the way of love …

TUESDAY, SIXTH WEEK OF LENT

O Lord, you have searched me and known me.

Psalm 139:1 (NRSV)

Praying with Psalm 139

You, O Holy One, you created me,
that's why you know me so well.

You are with me when I go to bed and when I get up;
you know what I am thinking wherever I am.

You have followed me wherever I have gone;
you know all the hurtful things and any good I may have done.

All the words I say you already know,
so why do you let me say them?
Because you are not a controller, like me?

I have turned away and ignored you,
but it does not make any difference to you;
you have always been there.

When I do great and good things you are there;
when I say rude and hurtful things or do selfish and shameful things,
you are there.

Look at me again, at all my hurtful ways,
and turn my feelings of regret into hopefulness,
that I may walk another way, moving closer to you.

Prayer moment

Read through Psalm 139 slowly. Stop when you stumble on a passage or word, and stay there. The ancient ones said that that is where God is speaking to you. What might God be saying to you? Rewrite each verse in your own words. Listen and open your heart to God's love.

Yes, Lord, you know me. I get that. What I don't understand is where you are when I resort to my old ways and turn away from you. Guide me on this Lenten journey and turn me around when I head down those old pathways …

WEDNESDAY, SIXTH WEEK OF LENT

O Lord, our Sovereign,
  how majestic is your name in all the earth!

You have set your glory above the heavens.

Psalm 8:1 (NRSV)

O rising sun (Early morning on Holy Island/Lindisfarne)

Awaken me, O rising sun,
as pink shadows rise in your glory
casting hues of colour across the sky.
Your brightness shines through the trees
sending out rays of warmth and light.
All creation is called
to witness to your beauty.
Birds sing their morning chants,
flowers bow in the wind

opening their arms to you.
I bow, too, giving thanks and praise,
but when I lift my head
your lamp no longer shines.
Shadows of grey fill the day
and branches brace themselves against the wind.
All creation awakens
and looks again for your glory.

Prayer moment

Go wandering outside, or spend some time looking through pictures in a nature book. Spend a few minutes thinking of the natural sites that appeal to you most and ask yourself why. In your praying time, ask yourself: what about nature makes you feel that you belong? Why is it so hard to hold on to those feelings? As you close your Lenten prayer, thank God for revealing God's glory to you in the wonder of nature.

God of rising suns, bless this day as I enter and witness your creation; restore my faith that I may see you not only on warm sunny days, but also in grey skies and howling wind ...

THURSDAY, SIXTH WEEK OF LENT

I will sing to the Lord as long as I live;
  I will sing praise to my God while I have being.

Psalm 104:33 (NRSV)

The beauty of today

The nightmare of the past
cannot erase the beauty of today.

Memories will return
and force their way into the present.

Many things will burn a hole
right through your heart.

But not all of it
will turn your world upside down or make things fall apart.

There is more on the road ahead
to lead you on your way.

Nothing can erase
the beauty of today.

Bless the Lord, O my soul.
Praise the Lord!

Prayer moment

Find a place, outside or inside, where you can sit and listen. Find a bit of nature or an indoor plant to observe. Look at the details and think of a few words of praise. Repeat those words several times during the day to thank God for the beauty of nature on your Lenten journey.

O Beauty of my heart, I stand before you, help me give you thanks and sing your praises for the blessings of your love, in this moment and in this place …

FRIDAY, SIXTH WEEK OF LENT

For the mountains may depart
  and the hills be removed,
but my steadfast love shall not depart from you,
  and my covenant of peace shall not be removed,
  says the Lord, who has compassion on you.

Isaiah 54:10 (NRSV)

All that matters

Peace is all that matters now,
broken hearts need time to heal,
wounded spirits cannot soar
when life's torn curtain hangs there still.

Peace is all that matters
in the silence of the heart.
Let love hold you now,
the One who called you here is with you still.

Love is here, see it there in the flame
flickering in the candlelight,
casting shadows on the wall.
See it shining through the window there
painted with its sacred story.

Peace is all that matters now,
hold the silence in your heart.
Give the world its noise clamouring to be heard,
and let love hold you now,
for peace is all that matters.

Prayer moment

How might you be God's peace today? What might you do as this Lenten season comes to an end to bring God's peace to those close to you? To the world?

Creator and Source of all blessings, bless me this day that I may be your peace and see your peace in others …

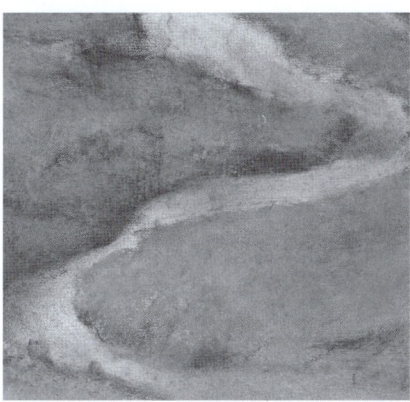

SATURDAY, SIXTH WEEK OF LENT

... let the field exult, and everything in it.
Then shall all the trees of the forest sing for joy
　before the Lord; for he is coming,
　for he is coming to judge the earth.
He will judge the world with righteousness,
　and the peoples with his truth.

Psalm 96:12–13 (NRSV)

Creation's song

Then creation's song goes heavenward
sending hope to rescue us,
catching melodies in our hearts to hear
the songs that cannot cease,
words that rise from deepest cries.

The world must answer for its crimes:
we all stand before the court
judging what we knew and when we knew it,
what we did and why we waited.

Over chaos and division
sounds of trumpets clamour through,
angels sing of harmony.
Heaven on earth will echo with songs of peace;
the celestial chorus will rise again,
when the world reclaims creation's song
praising love instead of hate.

Prayer moment

As part of your Lenten 'fast' make a list of some of the organisations near you that work for justice. Pray for each of these organisations and ask God to help you find one thing that you can do during Lent to help, such as volunteering or donating money or supplies. Invite others to join you. Pray to God to show you how to be more like Christ.

God of all creation, show us how to right the wrongs that destroy the earth and her glory, humans and their goodness …

HOLY WEEK

PALM/PASSION SUNDAY

Liturgy of the Palms

'Hosanna to the Son of David!
  Blessed is the one who comes in the name of the Lord!
Hosanna in the highest!'

Matthew 21:9 (NRSV)

(Read Matthew 21:1–10; Matthew 26; Luke 19:28–40)

A living remembrance

A living remembrance, a Eucharist,
each one of us: taken, blessed, broken, given.
Grace poured out to be shared with all the world,
a living sacrifice, held in the heart of goodness.

This is the day the Lord has made;
we will rejoice and be glad in it. (Ps 118:24, NRSV)

Blessed is the One who comes in the name of the Lord.
Hosanna in the highest!

Prayer moment

During the pandemic I really missed the Holy Week services in church: waving the palms, draping the cross, washing feet, breaking bread together … If possible, attend a worship service and read through the liturgies for Palm/Passion Sunday. These scripture passages contain a wide range of images and emotions. Place palm or pine branches and a cross near your bowl of sand/soil, as a reminder of Jesus' journey to the cross. Spend time reflecting on your Lenten journey and how today marks a transition for the coming week.

Blessed One, we give thanks for Holy Week celebrations and remembrance of you giving yourself to us. Blessed is the One who comes in the name of the Lord. Hosanna in the highest! …

Liturgy of the Passion

And the people stood by, watching; but the leaders scoffed at him, saying, 'He saved others; let him save himself if he is the Messiah of God, his chosen one!'

Luke 23:35 (NRSV)

(Read Luke 22:14–23:56)

My responsibility

Two thousand miles
two thousand years
two thousand tears
stretch across the universe and
nothing separates you from me.

All the goodness
all the acts of kindness
all the right decisions
will never come to be
unless I make them part of me.

Walking away
pointing fingers

ignoring suffering
all of this is part of me,
my responsibility.

Prayer moment

Pray and reflect on the Passion liturgy. Where do you see Pilate in the world today? In what ways are you part of the crowd? Who are you walking away from? Sit quietly and meditate on your journey through Lent and our entrance into Holy Week. What practical action for justice and peace might you take?

Voice of the voiceless, today I will not be quiet when I see injustice. I will not seek to please the crowd and abandon what is right and good …

MONDAY IN HOLY WEEK

Mary took a pound of costly perfume made of pure nard, anointed Jesus' feet, and wiped them with her hair. The house was filled with the fragrance of the perfume.

John 12:3 (NRSV)

Becoming a prayer

The smell of sweet perfume permeates the room.
Jesus is moving closer to the cross and so are we.
Mary reminds us of this in her humble act,
more costly than the perfume she brings.
What woman dare touch the Lord?

But he said, 'Leave her alone.'
She is the prayer he needs.

Could I become a prayer?
Taking hope to the hopeless,
pouring grace on the lost and lonely,
breaking bread with the hungry,
becoming a blessing.

Could I become a prayer?
Anointing Jesus' feet,
becoming a blessing
that flows from my heart,
spirit to spirit.
Freely given, asking nothing in return,
receiving the fragrance of life and love,
becoming a prayer.

Prayer moment

Ponder Mary's faithfulness and reflect on her love for Jesus (read John 12:1–8). Light some incense or pour some fragrant oil into a bowl of water; pray as the fragrance fills the room. What is your greatest struggle in becoming a prayer that someone needs; in giving your heart to the One who invites you ever closer? How will you mark this Holy Week? What act of mercy can you offer?

Companion of mercy, you call me to do what others will not do; turn my heart to those in need, teach me your mercy, strengthen me in your love …

TUESDAY IN HOLY WEEK

Judas, who betrayed him, said, 'Surely not I, Rabbi?' He replied, 'You have said so.'

Matthew 26:25 (NRSV)

And so, we wait

And so, we wait:
wait for Easter morning,
wait to end this fast,
wait for Thursday's supper
and the kiss of betrayal,
wait for the last words on Friday
and the cry from the cross,
wait.

Then the empty tomb ...
wait for the sun to rise,
wait for hope to fill our hearts,
wait for love to hold our hands,
wait for joy to enter our lives,
wait for peace to come,
wait to leave this wilderness,
wait.

Prayer moment

Spring-cleaning has a long tradition in Lent, in the preparing for Easter. Homes were cleaned and leaven removed. Churches were cleaned and altars washed. In your Easter waiting, remember this tradition by spring-cleaning your home, or volunteering to clean and polish the altar in a church or the tables in a nursing home. Do your cleaning with prayerful intention, turning your waiting into a sacred act of working. Pray for forgiveness for all the ways you may have devalued certain types of work, and for how you have betrayed Jesus.

Peace Bringer, when I turn away from your love and discredit the holiness of waiting, let the ordinary sounds of life unsettle me and keep me from betraying the blessings you bring in waiting and working. Help me honour you by honouring the work of others …

WEDNESDAY IN HOLY WEEK

He said, 'Abba, Father, for you all things are possible; remove this cup from me; yet, not what I want, but what you want.'

Mark 14:36 (NRSV)

Take this cup away

I cannot take this cup away.
I cannot rescue you.

The joy that once was here has vanished
as once it came.
The grief you feel is sorrow's way
and it too will disappear.

But for now,
I cannot take this cup away.
I cannot rescue you.

When you weep I will weep,
and as you wait I will wait.

For joy will return,
and grief will vanish
as once it came.

Prayer moment

For today's prayer, hold your favourite cup or mug. Look at its colour and shape. What do you like about it? Think of times of joy and sorrow when you have held this cup. When did you last experience joy or sorrow in your life? Hold your cup as you lift your prayers to God. Thank God for filling your cup and for being with you in times of sorrow and joy.

Amma Mother, Abba Father, hear my cries and the cries of broken people everywhere; and when we have cried our last tears, turn our cries into joy ...

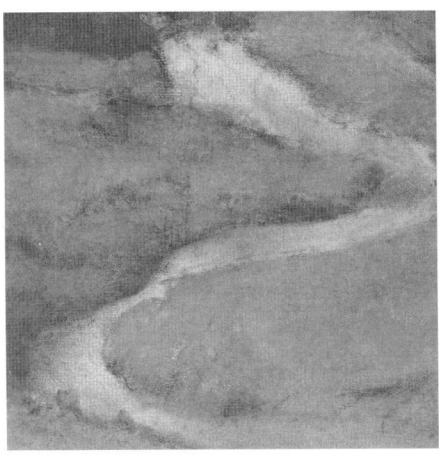

HOLY THURSDAY

I will greatly rejoice in the Lord,
  my whole being shall exult in my God;
for he has clothed me with the garments of salvation,
  he has covered me with the robe of righteousness,
as a bridegroom decks himself with a garland,
  and as a bride adorns herself with her jewels.

Isaiah 61:10 (NRSV)

Garment of fear

I wear a garment of fear
when the shroud of death is near.
Wearing fear I armour myself
against the thing I cannot face.
Yet death will come
as it will for everyone;
its mystery will engulf me and I will succumb
as others have done.

The rush of whispers in the wind,
a wave of voices from the past,
memories of sweet encounters,
none of that will last
when the looming robe of fear surrounds me.
It presses down upon my skin
and leaves me gasping for each breath.
Nothing lifts the heaviness
when I wear this garment.

Death's illusion has taken hold
and blocks my view of greener hills and bluer skies.

I walk into the mist,
stepping into the mystery;
I feel the hold of fear release its grip upon my soul.
Fear will not let me go, if I feed it with my agony.
I breathe the breath of God,
the garment falls away; piece by piece
it starts to tear, the threads unravel,
it cannot be mended now.
Little by little the weight is gone,
lifting me and moving on.

Prayer moment

If possible, participate in a Holy/Maundy Thursday service. Share in a Eucharist or Communion, or remember the Last Supper with a holy meal of your own bread and drink (not as a consecration of the elements but as a remembrance of the blessing). Read the Gospel lesson for today (John 13:1–17, 31b–35) and reflect on your journey through Lent. Ask God to help you through your own fears and stress.

O Risen One, Conqueror of death, reach into my fear and lift my anxious heart, that I may be wrapped in the robe of your peace and comfort …

GOOD FRIDAY

So Judas brought a detachment of soldiers together with police from the chief priests and the Pharisees, and they came there with lanterns and torches and weapons.

John 18:3 (NRSV)

Red Lantern of light

Red Lantern in the morning sky,
rising through barren trees,
scattering your light to greet another day,
fill our souls with life,
bring hope in the rising sun,
and light our way again.

Red Lantern in the evening sky,
benediction for another day,
night comes in your fading glow,
blowing wind through silent leaves,
give rest to weary souls.

Red Lantern of light,
falling into night,
bring peace that passes understanding,
until morning dawns
and another day comes.

Red Lantern of light,
break the spell of night,
scatter the shadows that linger still,

shine rays of hope
and light our way again.

Prayer moment

Make a rota of hours (a block of time between Good Friday evening and Easter Sunday morning) and invite people to sign up to pray for an hour. A special prayer space can be set up in the church, or elsewhere, and the lights left on with someone on duty; provide different prayer items such as a Bible and prayer books, candles, prayer beads, holding crosses, bowls of sand and water, crayons or coloured pencils and paper ... Some people are not familiar with this practice, so take time to encourage and guide their participation.

Light of all light, guide us through the shadows that linger in our world. Help us find ways to reach out to each other as we prepare to receive the joy of your resurrection ...

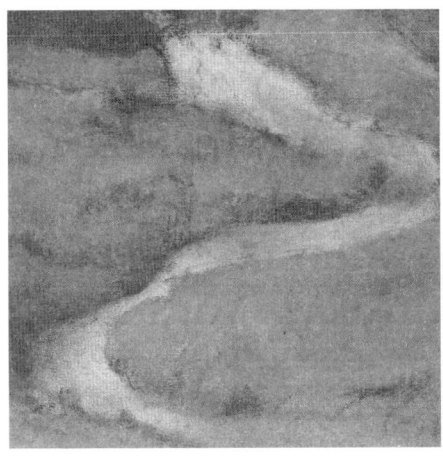

HOLY SATURDAY

'For there is hope for a tree,
  if it is cut down, that it will sprout again,
  and that its shoots will not cease ...'

Job 14:7 (NRSV)

Another Survivor Tree

Come, come to the wailing wall.
Come to where the Tree of Life stands tall,
where memories are held
and prayers were felled.
> Come, come to the centre.
> Oh come and let love enter.
> See the place where life met death,
> feel the presence of each last breath.

Come, come and face the truth.
Come and bring your youth.
Praise to Yahweh.
Praise each day.
> Come, come and bring your tears.
> Oh come and leave your fears.
> Hold high the banner of life
> for love will conquer every strife.

Another tree survived this way,
she stood while towers crumbled down that day.
The smoke rose and ashes fell
covering the terror that came from hell.

> Go, go to that Survivor Tree.
> Go and take your brokenness from here.
> Leave the pain that meets you there
> touching memory in the air.

Go to the Survivor Tree.
Oh go and live in what you see.
Watch her leaves as they fall,
see the remnants one and all.

> Come, oh come as the smoke rises,
> for the Tree of Life has no disguises.
> Go, go and see what is yet to be,
> another Survivor Tree.

Prayer moment

In 2001, the World Trade Towers were destroyed in New York City and thousands of people died. After the rubble was cleared, a small tree was found standing: named Survivor Tree, it is growing still.

In 2018, a gunman at a Jewish Synagogue, Tree of Life in Pittsburgh, Pennsylvania, killed 11 people and wounded six during Sabbath services. Guns claim the lives of thousands of people each year. Sometimes it feels like there is nothing we can do to stop the violence.

Find a news article about violence in your community/area and set it before you. Pray for the victims and their families and friends. Prayer is always a place to begin and end.

Survivor of evil, bless the good that rises still, that we may not be crushed but cling to hope that lives and will never die ...

EASTER SUNDAY

So the other disciples told him, 'We have seen the Lord.' But he said to them, 'Unless I see the mark of the nails in his hands, and put my finger in the mark of the nails and my hand in his side, I will not believe.'

John 20:25 (NRSV)

A moment of resurrection

A butterfly landed on me today,
while I sat there, under the tree.
I was surprised and tried not to breathe,
while it rested there, with wings outstretched –
orange and yellow, bright colours on display.
A butterfly landed on me today
as I struggled in silence, waiting and listening for God to show up.
I breathed and stared in awe.

A butterfly landed on me today
and calmed my worried soul, and slowed my anxious heart.
The heaviness of that light and gentle thing
rested there in the slowness of my breathing.
Its weight held me still, saying: rest and listen.
God is where you are, God is here, not over there.

I watched the butterfly that landed on me, mesmerised
by its presence,
held in awe by its weightlessness, resting there on me.
I stared watching, my chest rising and falling as I breathed.
The butterfly that landed on me

calmed my worried soul, and slowed my anxious heart.
A butterfly landed on me today
and I saw beauty, and I saw God,
a moment of resurrection,
amazing grace
in the weight of life.

Prayer moment

When, where have you experienced little or big moments of resurrection in your life? Where have you witnessed resurrection in the world? If you are with other people today, ask each person to draw a butterfly, then together share your drawings and stories of resurrection, revival or renewal. End by praying and thanking God for Christ's resurrection.

O Beauty of butterflies, release my doubt, renew my soul that I may encounter your resurrection throughout the coming Easter season ...

THE EASTER SEASON

SECOND SUNDAY OF EASTER

Now it was Mary Magdalene, Joanna, Mary the mother of James, and the other women with them who told this to the apostles. But these words seemed to them an idle tale, and they did not believe them.

Luke 24:10–11 (NRSV)

She carries the light

She carries the light wherever she goes.
She cannot hide who she is.
She is who she is.
She swims in light, like a fish in water.
She is who she is.
She calms the seas and the air with her light.
She lives the holy life
and follows the way of the Christ.
She is one of Three,
the Spirit of Trinity.

Yet, we cannot see her
because we look elsewhere
for someone more important,
someone bigger and better,
louder and more powerful.
It is a shame,
because we miss the light
when she is gone.

Prayer moment

Who are the women who have influenced your life? In what ways did they affirm you? Find a picture or photograph of a woman who has influenced you; it could be a biblical or historical woman or a family member or friend. Or picture someone in your mind. Pray that her faithfulness might help you through the Great Fifty Days after Easter. Send notes of appreciation to women working in your community to make a difference in the lives of others.

O Spirit of light, God of man and woman, Christ in all that is, let your image shine through us today, that we may not miss your presence when you come to us …

THE DAY OF PENTECOST

And suddenly from heaven there came a sound like the rush of a violent wind, and it filled the entire house where they were sitting.

Acts 2:2 (NRSV)

> **Spirit comes**
>
> One season ends,
> another begins.
> In the silence
> comes a sound,
> life is always breaking through.
> Listen,
> Spirit comes.

The day is over now,
another rushes in.
In the silence
hear the sound
breaking through.
Listen,
Spirit comes.

Finding our way back,
praying our way forward,
there is a new beginning.
In the silence
hold the sound
filling all around.
Listen,
Spirit comes.

Prayer moment

In quiet contemplation, listen for the sounds around you. What do you hear? Rather than trying to push the sounds away as noise, receive them, imagine where they are coming from. Pray for the those who are making them. Ask the Spirit to fill you with compassion for sounds or voices that annoy you.

Now think of the sounds and voices that bring you joy. Ask the Spirit to fill you with peace and understanding for the days ahead.

Breath of Life, Winds of the Spirit, renew us with the warmth of your love and fill our homes with sounds of joy, of Pentecost moments, that we may be your peace in the world …

PRAYER MOMENTS IN OUR ADVENT WAITING:

Christ the King Sunday to Christmas and beyond

Introduction

Many people say they are too busy to set aside valuable time to pray, but even a few seconds, with or without words, can help us to catch our breath and defuse some of the stress that finds its way into our minds and bodies. No matter what season we are in, prayer connects us with the rest of the world and provides a conduit to the Holy for our concerns about all that is happening around us. Choosing prayer does not negate our efforts for social action nor mean we have given up on working to make a difference in the world. In fact, prayer is social action, a positive response to negative forces, whether sitting quietly or working diligently. It is active engagement in what is happening around us, asking the Divine to intercede with us, so together we can make 'peace on earth' a reality, not a cliché.

During the Covid days, I began sewing facemasks and donating them to charities. Sewing became a prayerful process in which I felt connected to those who were risking their lives on the frontlines in order to keep others safe. This slowly evolved into another project which I called 'Covid Challenge: Sew seeds of kindness'. I used fabric leftover from the masks and made clergy stoles (to match the masks) for ordained women and sent them as gifts. The intention was that they would receive a surprise in the post with a note that thanked them for their ministry and reminded them that we are all connected by the same threads of destiny, and that their ministry makes a difference in building God's beloved community. After receiving numerous thank you notes, I know that the project has blessed many women who feel alone on the frontlines of the church. In the end, though, it has been a blessing for me.

There are as many ways of praying as there are of reaching out to others. The prayerful act of sewing inspires me to encourage others to do something to keep hope alive in small acts of kindness. It might be phoning someone, or simply saying 'thank you' to store clerks, or writing one 'thinking of you' note every day to someone in your church or community.

As we enter this Advent season and prepare for another Christmas, what might you do to offer a gift of kindness to someone? What about shovelling snow or delivering a meal without being asked? Volunteering to grocery shop or to drive someone to a doctor appointment? Offering to babysit so parents can do errands or spend a quiet evening together? Walking dogs? Picking up litter? Housecleaning? Volunteering at food banks or shelters? The possibilities are all around us for ordinary, everyday acts of kindness which become extraordinary when they are given. Each of us can do something for the beloved community. Nothing can keep us from loving what God loves, sowing seeds of kindness, finding our way back and praying our way forward in all seasons of our lives.

Rebeka Maples

Note:

Read about the sewing project at: 'Columbus woman sends gifts to female Methodist pastors', The Columbus Dispatch, https://eu.dispatch.com

CHRIST THE KING SUNDAY

*Let your priests be clothed with righteousness,
 and let your faithful shout for joy.*

Psalm 132:9 (NRSV)

Sewing seeds of kindness

Weaving time through the fabric of life,
sewing seeds of kindness
by design and redesign,
torn and tattered,
used and new,
sewing seams together,
separated by colour,
drawn into patterns.

The weaver weaves,
the sewer sews,
one stitch at a time,
overlapping strands,
tearing out, starting over.

By design or redesign
the threads of life
are intertwined,
each stitch needs the other
to hold the pieces
together.

Prayer moment

This poem was included with the stoles and facemasks that I sent to clergy-women (see p.104). What might you plan to do for someone during Advent that is not expected? In your prayers, ask God to help you choose an idea, then sit quietly and jot down any plans that come to you.

God who clothed creation, mend the threads of our lives and bring the people of the earth, who are divided by war and hate, together into your beloved community; bind us together with threads that cannot be broken …

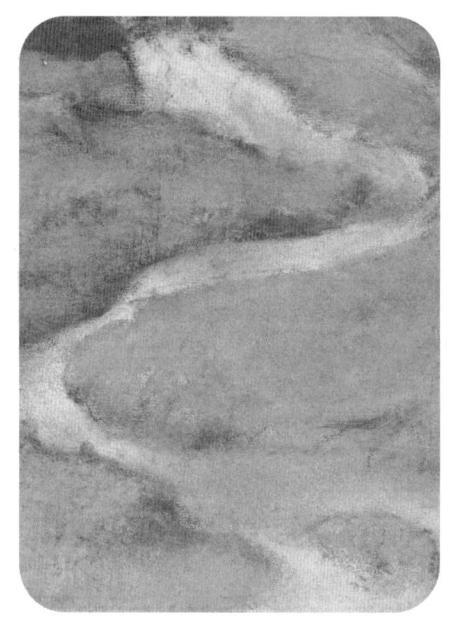

FIRST WEEK OF ADVENT

SUNDAY, FIRST WEEK OF ADVENT

O, house of Jacob,
  come, let us walk
  in the light of the Lord!

Isaiah 2:5 (NRSV)

Advent hope

Today, we light the first Advent candle,
a candle of hope,
looking for the coming of a Star Child,
thinking back to the rising of a Christ Child,
our hope now and forever.

In hope, we look forward, thinking back,
celebrating the risen light.
We think back, looking forward to the coming light,
praying for hope to find a home in our lives.

Prayer moment

Make an Advent wreath with evergreen branches and five candles (real or battery-powered). Place four coloured candles, one for each Sunday, in the circle of the wreath, and a white one, the Christ candle, in the centre for Christmas Day. Begin your prayers each day this week by lighting the first candle.

Light of Advent, I pray that you will shine the light of hope into my heart and the heart of the world during this Advent season ...

MONDAY, FIRST WEEK OF ADVENT

Then he told them a parable: 'Look at the fig tree and all the trees; as soon as they sprout leaves you can see for yourselves and know that summer is already near. So also, when you see these things taking place, you know that the kingdom of God is near.'

Luke 21:29–31 (NRSV)

In the waiting

Silent movement
hear the sound.
Angels singing
all around.
Star that rises
into light.
Holy manger
shining bright.

Silent sound
all around.
Listening in
slowing down.
Grace that changes
old to new.
Speaks in silence
calling you.

Prayer moment

As you begin this first week of Advent, find a moment to go outside and feel the warm breeze or cold wind on your face. Be still for a moment and breathe in new life; breathe out tension and anxiety … breathe in … breathe out …

Breath of changing seasons, I feel flowing air and know that it is a sign of you breathing new life into the world again; come in the silent moments of this day and restore your breath in me …

TUESDAY, FIRST WEEK OF ADVENT

And why has this happened to me, that the mother of my Lord comes to me? …

Luke 1:43 (NRSV)

Mystery of light

In Elizabeth's house,
Mary sings her song of praise,
'My soul magnifies the Lord.'

Filled with the light of peace,
bearer of the Son of God
born human through her love.

Mystery of light in the flesh
she carries the gift,
delivering life and light to all the world.

> Introducing One of Three into our lives,
> bearer of the light sings her song of praise,
> first disciple, giving birth to her prayer of grace.

Prayer moment

Advent comes from the Latin word *Adventus* (the 'coming' adventure) and is a time of waiting with expectation and hope. There is much excitement and anticipation in the preparations for Christmas, but unfortunately a lot of it these days is commercial, with companies eager to take our money by playing on our weaknesses and tempting us to buy more and more to try to capture the magic of Christmas. What Christmas traditions do you value most? How might you spend less money this year and instead enjoy more of the spirit and adventure of Christmas?

Mother of God, pray for me as I remember your gift of grace …

WEDNESDAY, FIRST WEEK OF ADVENT

Our help is in the name of the Lord,
who made heaven and earth.

Psalm 124:8 (NRSV)

> **Hope calls**
>
> Hope calls through the night
> on bells that ring
> and choirs that sing.

Never stop ringing.
Never stop singing.

Hope comes in nightbird songs
while the world sleeps,
sending messages of peace,
echoing through the silent air.

Hope ushers in a new day
giving grace room for blessing
and mercy time for healing.
Endless.
Everlasting.
Hope brings us home
on songs in the night.

Prayer moment

What are you hoping for this Christmas? What do you long for in your life? Spend time writing prayers or talking to God about your hopes and longings. Plan one thing you can do to start to make them happen. End your prayers by reading or singing the words of a Christmas song.

Come my Hope, my Light, my Life, come to me in my Advent waiting. Bring hope to my heart and your fullness to my life. Bring your promise to our world, and open our mouths to sing and our minds to love …

THURSDAY, FIRST WEEK OF ADVENT

Blessed be the Lord, the God of Israel,
  who alone does wondrous things.
Blessed be his glorious name forever;
  may his glory fill the whole earth.
Amen and Amen.

Psalm 72:18–19 (NRSV)

Moving into Christmas

Light falling into Christmas,
snow floating through the air,
gently moving on the ground.

Then suddenly, without warning,
it all turned around,
upside was down, outside was in,
waiting changed.
Candlelighting and carol-singing
thrown online, into cyberspace.

Virtually we met,
voyeurs watching each other,
lighting, singing,
waiting still, keeping watch,
pilgrims moving into Christmas.

Prayer moment

In 2019, the coronavirus changed the world, changed our lives, changed our worship. What upset you most when the virus spread and we were forced to social distance? What are some positive things that came out of the situation? Think of times when you felt God's presence and were able to experience the wonder of God's love. Thank God for being present with us in all things and at all times.

God of wonder, God of coming marvels, shine your light and open my eyes when I cannot see the beauty of your presence …

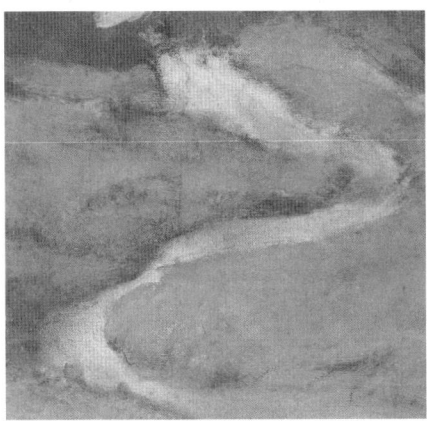

FRIDAY, FIRST WEEK OF ADVENT

'Look, the virgin shall conceive and bear a son,
  and they shall name him Emmanuel,'
which means, "God is with us".

Matthew 1:23 (NRSV)

Christmas is coming

Christmas is coming,
amazing grace, how sweet the sound
telling us that Christ is near.

Now is our time
to receive the gift,
for Christmas comes
to kiss our lives.

It will return again next year
but Christ will never leave.
God is with us
even as we wait.
Christmas comes again this year.

Christ will bring the gift we need,
and so we wait
for Christmas coming
to kiss our lives again.

Prayer moment

What is the best Christmas gift you've ever received? Thank God for the giver. Think of one special gift that you could give to someone that would not require a lot of money. Start working on ways to make that happen.

Giver of all gifts, what offering can I give when I have the gift of your amazing grace, poured out for me again and again …

SATURDAY, FIRST WEEK OF ADVENT

Our soul waits for the Lord;
  he is our help and shield …
Let your steadfast love, O Lord, be upon us,
  even as we hope in you.

Psalm 33:20, 22 (NRSV)

Winter brings hope

Winter brings hope.
No matter how faint our vision, how low our feelings,
this harsh and mysterious season brings hope.
Listen and you will hear
dreams opening in frozen crystals,
beauty glittering through barren trees,
whispers coming from angels near.

Winter bears hope
in seeds of life buried deep,

as nature prepares for sleep
in this waiting time.
All is gathered in,
creation rests
until spring bursts forth
ushering in all the resurrections that winter brings.

Prayer moment

Think about what you find beautiful and hopeful about the winter season: seeds waiting underground; trees without their leaves standing strong in the wind; the encompassing, cosy blanket of longer nights … Pray with these images and lift up those who struggle in the cold or through being alone. May our prayers bring hope.

Companion of winter nights, as I prepare for the coming season, may my heart be nurtured in your care, waiting for all the possibilities Christ brings into my life …

SECOND WEEK OF ADVENT

SUNDAY, SECOND WEEK OF ADVENT

But the angel said to them, 'Do not be afraid; for see – I am bringing you good news of great joy for all the people …'

Luke 2:10 (NRSV)

Advent joy

Today, we light the second Advent candle,
a candle of joy.
The angel told the shepherds
about a birth that would bring great joy,
a sign from God for all people.

In joy, we wait for the birth of a Child,
one who delivers new life into our lives,
one who brings good news
and sends angels to bless us through all our fears and sadness.

Prayer moment

Light two of your Advent candles; light these two candles each day this week before your prayers. Do you have any holiday traditions of preparing or eating special dinners or sweet treats? If you are able, prepare a meal or bake some treats, and ask a friend to join you to enjoy some time together; or take the food to a neighbour, just to bring a little joy into someone's life.

God of Advent Joy, come into my heart today, and help me share your good news with others …

MONDAY, SECOND WEEK OF ADVENT

But let justice roll down like waters,
  and righteousness like an ever-flowing stream.

Amos 5:24 (NRSV)

Remember water

I remember water
blessed and holy
rolling down with righteousness.
I remember bread
given for the life of the world.
I remember wine
poured out for forgiveness of sins.
Oh, I remember
the Word was life,
the light of the world.
I remember justice
rolling down like a mighty stream.
And I remember the tiny seed
growing into the greatest tree
dying on a cross for me.

We know water
because we were born in water.
We bathe in it and drink it.
We know water
because it gives us life
and restores all living things.
Yes, we know water.

> Baptised and birthed in it,
> marked by it
> and sealed by it,
> forever blessed
> and always beloved
> descending from above.

Prayer moment

Water plays a significant role throughout the scriptures, from Noah and the flood and Moses parting the Red Sea to Jesus' baptism. Set a bowl or glass of water near you and touch the water or take a drink. Consult various websites: WaterAid, Action Against Hunger, Oxfam … Carry God's love and justice into the world by acting to help protect the earth's water.

O God of light, come to me in my Advent waiting; let me see the waters of life, that I may carry your love into the world …

TUESDAY, SECOND WEEK OF ADVENT

Then God said, 'Let there be light'; and there was light.

Genesis 1:3 (NRSV)

Light enters

Light enters at sunrise
and disappears at sunset.
It lifts the heavy soul
and chases darkness away.
Light floods in
and changes night to day
connects everything everywhere.

Light bears our burdens while we sleep,
grows our food so we can eat,
guiding our way,
shining on our path,
everything connected everywhere at once.

Prayer moment

Light your two Advent candles and focus on them; or open the curtains and sit and watch the sun move across the room. How might you help to bring light to those who are living in darkness, those on the streets or struggling with depression?

Light of all that is, you have always been and will be until night comes and you shine somewhere else. For now, in this time we have together, I will receive the gift you bring and give you thanks for light and life and all that is …

WEDNESDAY, SECOND WEEK OF ADVENT

But Ruth said,

'Do not press me to leave you
 or to turn back from following you!
Where you go, I will go;
 where you lodge, I will lodge;
your people shall be my people,
 and your God my God …'

Ruth 1:16 (NRSV)

Sing a song

Sing a song of thanksgiving
for all that came and is yet to be,
for days of joy and peace,
for times of sadness too, and grief.

Sing songs of goodness
for all that feeds the soul,
for beauty on country lanes and city streets,
for friendships that weather storms.

Sing the song that's in your heart
with all the love you have,
with grace that overflows
and mercy that you have known.
Sing a song and give thanks!

Prayer moment

What is your favourite Christmas carol? Find the words and read or sing each line as a prayer, feeling the joy that these words bring to your heart. Remember a friend who has brought joy into your life and send her/him a Christmas card of thanks for their friendship. You might write the words of the song in your card.

Holy One of God, hear me as I sing my thanks to you; help me in my struggles to have faith like Ruth's and trust in the messengers you send to guide me ever closer to you …

THURSDAY, SECOND WEEK OF ADVENT

For where your treasure is, there your heart will be also.

Matthew 6:21 (NRSV)

Gift of gold

Music follows the sound when it stops,
silence is gold, a gift of old.

But silence cannot be held or stored on the shelf,
locked behind doors or switched on and off,
placed in a box or sung by a choir.

Silence is held where music lives,
with all other treasures inside the heart.

Prayer moment

Read the verse and poem again, then sit in silence for a while. How will you honour the world today with the gifts God has given you?

Treasure of all treasures, come into my heart and help me to honour you this Christmas with gifts greater than gold ...

FRIDAY, SECOND WEEK OF ADVENT

There are many who say, 'O that we might see some good!
  Let the light of your face shine on us, O Lord!'

Psalm 4:6 (NRSV)

Light on a silent stage

At the end of the dock,
a lone crane
descends suddenly from the sky,
hovering, then landing, wings extended,
standing with
neck outstretched,
balancing on one foot.
In the light of the setting sun,
the feathered dancer scans life across the water.

Nature watching over creation
stops to clean the day's dust away,
working diligently as if preparing for a final curtain call,
crouched in upon itself, resting on one foot,
neck hidden now in a plumage mound.
At the end of the mooring place,
feathers rippling in the wind,
waves beating in steady rhythm against the dock,
a soundless message comes in winged form
as light falls on a silent stage.

Prayer moment

What are you feeling anxious or good about today? Sit and offer your feelings to God; whatever they are, know that God can handle them. Continue to sit quietly; write a few Christmas cards while you listen to Christmas music.

Peacemaker, during this holy season of Advent, renew me with strength enough to be still and experience quiet moments, knowing you will be with me in all my joy and sadness ...

SATURDAY, SECOND WEEK OF ADVENT

By day the Lord commands his steadfast love,
  and at night his song is with me,
  a prayer to the God of my life.

Psalm 42:8 (NRSV)

In Advent waiting

Hail to the waiting light.
Hail to the One of Hope.

Hail to the falling light.
Hail to the Child of Love.

Hail to the coming light.
Hail to the birth of Joy.

Hail to the rising light.
Hail to the way of Peace.

God, be with me in my waiting:
In my memories, God, be there.
In my emptiness, God, be there.
In my praying, God, be there.
In my sleeping and my waking, God, find me there.
Song of God, be with me.

Prayer moment

The Advent and Christmas season can be lonely. Contact a few friends and plan a time to get together, in person or on Zoom, to sing Christmas songs. You might even go carolling!

Song of life, sing to me in the day wherever I am and in the night when I sleep, that I may carry your love and hope into a waiting world ...

THIRD WEEK OF ADVENT

SUNDAY, THIRD WEEK OF ADVENT

So we have known and believe the love that God has for us.
God is love, and those who abide in love abide in God, and God abides in them.

1 John 4:16 (NRSV)

Advent love

Today we light the third candle,
a candle of love.
Love comes from God. Love is God and is one with God.
Love knows God and flows from God.
Love is understanding, all knowing, all in One.

In love, we pray for each other,
for those who have been hurt in the name of love,
and for those who search for love.
In the light of this candle, we pray for an understanding of love,
for God comes with angels to bless us and show us how to love.

Prayer moment

Light three of the Advent candles, then sit quietly; light these three candles each day this week before your prayers. Where did you see love this past week? Who are the angels in your life? Who has shown you how to love? Pray for these angels, and then slowly let your thoughts fall into silence.

Lover of all understanding, because you first loved us, we light this candle; help us to grow in understanding, that we may show others your love …

MONDAY, THIRD WEEK OF ADVENT

The angel replied, 'I am Gabriel. I stand in the presence of God, and I have been sent to speak to you and to bring you this good news …'

Luke 1:19 (NRSV)

The coming light

Morning calls to morning
as we awake from sleep.
The sun rises slowly
as the moon fades into the coming light.
Silence before the dawn has broken now
bringing a new day.

What awaits us in the coming hours?
What holiness will unfold in the birthing of the Word
and the opening of our minds?
Another day is dawning
when Wisdom enters in
bringing blessings from the coming light.

Prayer moment

Rise early and go out to watch the sunrise. If the sun is shining, feel the sun on your face. Close your eyes and thank God for the sun that brings beauty to the earth. What good news, what positive words can you help to bring to others, to the world, in this Advent season …

Spirit of holiness, I give thanks for the coming of your Wisdom that is born anew every morning …

TUESDAY, THIRD WEEK OF ADVENT

He went to be registered with Mary, to whom he was engaged and who was expecting a child.

Luke 2:5 (NRSV)

God of mystery

God of mystery, we greet you.
God of holy birth, we honour you.
God of migrant parents, we know you.
God of pain and suffering, have mercy on us.
God of the poor and hungry, we see you.
God of all who seek you, come and meet us.

Prayer moment

When you read stories in the news about refugees and those who are homeless do you ever think of the Holy Family? Find a way of connecting more with the marginalised people in your community and pray for them through the Advent season and beyond.

God of all who search and find a home, God of all who search and struggle still, bless each of us now, that we may see you in the struggles of others ...

WEDNESDAY, THIRD WEEK OF ADVENT

The wolf shall live with the lamb,
  the leopard shall lie down with the kid,
the calf and the lion and the fatling together,
  and a little child shall lead them.

Isaiah 11:6 (NRSV)

Extra-ordinary

The extra-ordinary is found in the ordinary.
Love is found in everyday moments.
I see the vastness of the cosmos
and the twinkling of a star,
everyday occurrences but nothing ordinary.
I see the snow falling, a flower blooming,
a child playing,
everyday blessings in ordinary events.
Birthed from an ordinary beginning
into something extra-ordinary, a Holy Child.
Sing praises to the One who is and was
and will be through the ages:
Adonai, Elohim, Shalom.

Prayer moment

In your Advent waiting and Christmas preparations, reflect on the ordinary, everyday gifts God blesses you with. Name them in your praying and carry them in your heart throughout the day and into your sleep.

Child of humble parents, you who lived in human form, come to us in our Advent waiting. Awaken us and show us once again how to live with the gift of your love in ordinary and extraordinary times ...

THURSDAY, THIRD WEEK OF ADVENT

Why are you cast down, O my soul,
  and why are you disquieted within me?
Hope in God; for I shall again praise him,
  my help and my God.

Psalm 42:11 (NRSV)

A blue Christmas

For some, Christmas is a painful season,
festivities and joyful gatherings feel empty and depressing,
in the story of a Holy Family.

The first Christmas without a loved one,
a time that holds memories of family tensions,
the anguish of broken relationships, insecurity and loss,
weariness of health problems, loneliness in isolation,
reminiscent of a Holy Family.

In the midst of all the celebrating,
a Blue Christmas wrapped in Eucharistic prayers
brings hope in remembering,
peace in exile,
benediction of a Holy Family.

Prayer moment

In your prayers, remember someone who might be lonely. Phone that person to say that you are thinking of them; don't try to fix their situation, just listen. Plan or attend a Blue Christmas service and invite someone to join you. Touch someone with kindness and you touch God.

O migrant Child, we cry in this time of joy, and wonder why happiness is so far away; come, that we may know the peace you bring ...

FRIDAY, THIRD WEEK OF ADVENT

And you, child, will be called the prophet of the Most High;
  for you will go before the Lord to prepare his ways ...

Luke 1:76 (NRSV)

Child with us

Come to us, Child of God, wake us from our sleep,
  lead us in your ways of mercy and peace.
Come to us, Child of Light, renew us with your love,
  mend our ways in the glow of your grace.
Come to us, Child of Love, meet us in our comfort and greed,
  call us out of ourselves and into your goodness.
Come to us, Child of Peace, see us on our streets and in our homes,
  guide us that our wars may be no more.
Come to us, Child with us, come and live among us,
  reveal your image in us.

Prayer moment

What Christmas memory from childhood do you hold dear? If there is a child in your life, plan to get together with them for a walk in the park or a time of play. Listen to that child and affirm their dreams.

Come to us, Emmanuel, be with us in our waiting, open us to the gift of your love and remain with us today, tomorrow and always ...

SATURDAY, THIRD WEEK OF ADVENT

'... to you is born this day in the city of David a Saviour, who is the Messiah, the Lord.'

Luke 2:11 (NRSV)

As the choir sings

As the choir sings 'Once in royal David's city'
the music floods over me,
the voices harmonise into One
telling me a star is coming, a light is born.

Here the voice of God has won my heart,
speaking over me, breathing in me,
gift from heaven all around
in its gentle lowly sound.

I feel the loving mother mild
laying me in that manger with her child;

the sweetness of the song fills the air
as angels sing another verse.

Tears roll down
and words tumble to the ground,
for that child so meek and mild
comes to lead his children home.

Prayer moment

What visual symbols of Christmas do you treasure most? Sit near the Christmas tree or the Nativity scene, or another Christmas item or decoration special to you, and listen to some Christmas music. Let the sound wash over you and lift any stress or tension you may be feeling. While the music plays, imagine yourself being held in God's love.

Holy One, divine and human, come into our weakness, shine your glory on us; let us see you in all our evensongs and morning prayers …

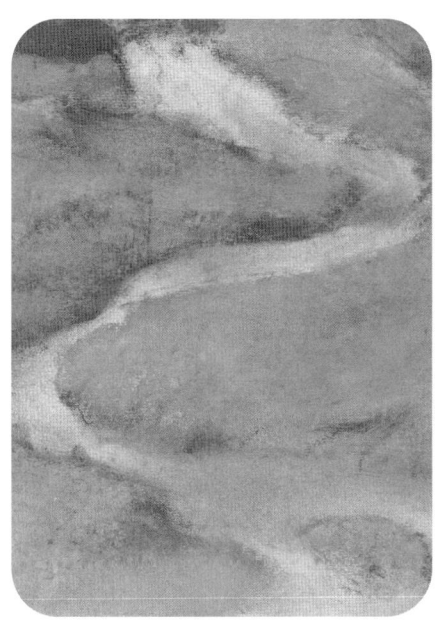

FOURTH WEEK OF ADVENT

SUNDAY, FOURTH WEEK OF ADVENT

And the peace of God, which surpasses all understanding, will guard your hearts and minds in Christ Jesus.

Philippians 4:7 (NRSV)

Advent peace

Today we light the fourth candle,
a candle of peace.
God came to earth as a Child to show us
peace on earth as in heaven.

In peace, we pray with anxious hearts,
naming places in our suffering world.
Loved and held together,
we weave our brokenness to God.
In Christ we pray
for the peace that brings all understanding.

Prayer moment

Light the four Advent candles today and each day this week before you pray. Sit quietly in your praying. Name places around the world where people are suffering. Pray for peace organisations and projects in your church or community, and for ways that you can help to bring peace to your neighbourhood and to the neighbourhood of the world.

Child of peace, you are so close, in us and around us; help us to be your peace in the world, with our prayers and in our actions ...

MONDAY, FOURTH WEEK OF ADVENT

And Mary said,

> *'My soul magnifies the Lord,*
> *and my spirit rejoices in God my Saviour …'*

Luke 1:46–47 (NRSV)

My spirit rejoices

What sings in your soul,
keeps you awake or lulls you to sleep?
Write it on your heart,
hold it in your prayer.
Rejoice for the Mother of God,
bearer of grace, presence of peace.
Mary sings and her song is for all of us.
Her love comes and when it does
joy returns singing in our souls,
'My spirit rejoices in God my Saviour.'
For the Holy One has done good things for us
and Holy is God's name,
Source of Love, Word of Love, Spirit of Love.

Prayer moment

What are some of the names you use for God? Most prayers and English translations of the Bible use only male pronouns for God, causing us to think of God as a person or male. Get together with a few friends and list your names for God. What words are familiar, or not so easy to use? As we move closer to Christmas, practise using different names for God in your prayers.

O Spirit of God-with-us in this place and in this time, renew us as followers of Christ, that the world might see and know your love through us ...

TUESDAY, FOURTH WEEK OF ADVENT

*The people who walked in darkness
   have seen a great light;
those who lived in a land of great darkness –
   on them light has shined.*

Isaiah 9:2 (NRSV)

Miracle and mystery

God of Christ and Christmas light,
you came into our lives as a helpless child,
you needed a family, someone to care for you.

God Child of Christmas light,
we stop to thank you for your never-ending miracle,
we stop to honour the mystery of your birth.

Christ Child of Christmas light,
you cried because you were hungry, because you were homeless,
because you were a stranger in a foreign land;
we cry when we are not there where you need us to be.

Prayer moment

Where does Christ need you to be? What are some of the shelters or organisations near you that serve people who are homeless? Contact one of them and find out what they most need this Christmas. Invite others to join you to donate or volunteer. Think about where else Christ needs you to be.

Star Child, in the silence of my prayer I thank you for the beauty of Christmas lights and the mystery that your birth awakens in me ...

WEDNESDAY, FOURTH WEEK OF ADVENT

'I will not leave you orphaned; I am coming to you. In a little while the world will no longer see me, but you will see me; because I live, you also will live ...'

John 14:18–19 (NRSV)

Like a flower

Like a flower breaking through concrete,
Peace comes.

Like a word that softens death,
Peace comes.

Like a song that shatters glass,
Peace comes.

Like silence that disturbs,
Peace comes.

Like rain that falls from above,
Peace descends.

Like a child born in exile,
Peace arrives.

Prayer moment

Write a letter of welcome to refugees in your community, or sign up to an online campaign supporting refugees' rights. Whenever we welcome the stranger, we welcome Christ.

Refugee Child, your peace comes in many ways; may we be wise enough to see and humble enough to understand all the ways you come to us …

THURSDAY, FOURTH WEEK OF ADVENT

And the Word became flesh and lived among us, and we have seen his glory, the glory as of a father's only son, full of grace and truth.

John 1:14 (NRSV)

Gift child

God of everlasting peace,
One who holds us in this holy time.

Come to us in the light of a star,
send your love from Heaven's Child.

Comfort us in this sacred season,
and we will share the glory when the feast is over.

In our waiting, we now pray:
God of nights cold and dark, bless us with your Gift Child.

Prayer moment

As Christmas draws near, allow yourself some time to dream as a child, to see and feel, once again, the wonder, magic and excitement of this time. Read to a child (or aloud to yourself) a child's Christmas story, or 'The night before Christmas'.

Child of truth and grace, you come each year asking nothing and giving everything; renew our hope in your never-ending gift of all and more ...

CHRISTMAS EVE

For a child has been born for us,
  a son given to us;
authority rests upon his shoulders;
  and he is named
Wonderful Counselor, Mighty God,
  Everlasting Father, Prince of Peace.

Isaiah 9:6 (NRSV)

Starlight

Star, star, quiet star
shining softly,
silent sparkle in the night.

Still, still, hear the star
lighting up the sky,
silent noise from afar.

Hush, hush, soundless stream
falling on the snow,
silent glimmer through the air.
Star, star, shine your light.

Prayer moment

Light your four Advent candles and the Christ candle. Set a nativity scene nearby. If you are able to, attend a Christmas Eve service, or watch one online. Let the scripture readings and songs be your prayer … receive the blessings the Christ child brings.

God of this holy night, shine with the brightness of your Light. Grant that we may carry your Mystery throughout the earth as in heaven, knowing that the light of your love lives in us through all our days …

CHRISTMAS DAY

While they were there, the time came for her to deliver her child. And she gave birth to her firstborn son and wrapped him in bands of cloth, and laid him in a manger, because there was no place for them in the inn.

Luke 2:6–7 (NRSV)

O Christmas Day, O Day of Christ

Each year you call us here,
each year we come,
tired now from twinkling lights and Christmas puddings,
and yet, we come,
hoping for a glimpse of you,
the Mystery, wrapped in children's laughter and winter's starlight.
Are you real?
My heart longs for you.
Will you touch the sadness, and heal the brokenness?
My heart longs to know.

The day arrives and you sneak in
amidst the joy and excitement, underneath the empty wrappings.
O Christmas Day, O Day of Christ,
you ring with news of a Child
born to set us free,

> born to save the world from ourselves.
> And so, we come,
> with longing hearts,
> to believe that such a thing is true.
> O Christmas Day, O Day of Christ.

Prayer moment

Light the four Advent candles and the Christ candle. Read Luke 2:1–20. Set the nativity scene, name each figure and say a prayer. What has the Advent and Christmas journey meant to you this year?

O Christ, we sing to you with gifts of love, praising you for all you bring. May you be born in us again this day, that your grace may be renewed in us throughout the year …

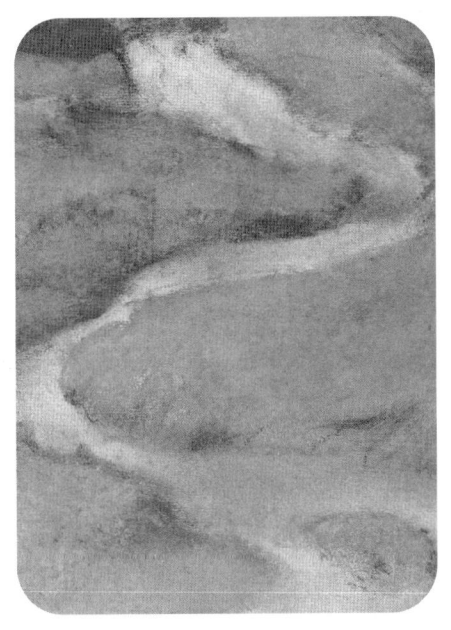

AFTER CHRISTMAS DAY

FIRST SUNDAY AFTER CHRISTMAS DAY

And when he was twelve years old, they went up as usual for the festival.

Luke 2:42 (NRSV)

Christmas is over

Suddenly Christmas is over.
Jesus is twelve years old, as the story is told.
He begins his preaching; we begin our whining.
The complaint is: Christmas season starts too early
and lasts too long.
It's too early because shopping starts weeks before Advent begins,
but how can it be too long,
since we sweep Christmas out the door as soon as it is over?

Christmas is over,
and the birth of God is still unwrapped,
the world is not at peace, the poor are still poor,
hungry children still cry,
war continues, and hate lives on.
Who will unwrap the gift?

Christmas is never over, not too early, not too long,
and peace still comes;
it lingers near
in the shadow of a cross.

Prayer moment

As you recover from all the excitement of Christmas and begin to hurry into cleaning and taking down the tree, stop for a moment and light your Christ candle again. Remember: the light of Christ never goes out. Wait instead until Epiphany (6th January), the traditional day for packing away Christmas, to take down your tree. Sing Christmas carols and ask yourself: where did you see Jesus and God this Christmas?

Child God, Prince of Peace, the celebration is over and I still long for starlit nights and angel voices. Please, open your gift in my heart ...

EPIPHANY OF THE LORD

Arise, shine; for your light has come,
  and the glory of the Lord has risen upon you.

Isaiah 60:1 (NRSV)

On entering the house, they saw the child with Mary his mother; and they knelt down and paid him homage. Then, opening their treasure chests, they offered him gifts of gold, frankincense, and myrrh.

Matthew 2:11 (NRSV)

Blessing

God of gold, frankincense and myrrh
bless us in your dawning light.
Guide us through these hallowed days.
Send us out with gifts of grace,
signs of peace and healing rays.

God of grace and mercy bright,
wrap us in the Spirit of your holy light.

Bless us now with eyes that see,
love and incense flowing free,
singing praises now to thee.
Yahweh Christ and Holy Mother,
Glory to Abba Lord.

Prayer moment

Epiphany (6th January) marks the end of the Christmas season, the twelfth day of Christmas. The Magi have arrived to announce our light has come. If you have not done so already, this is the day to take down all the Christmas decorations, pack them away and make room for God's light to fill your heart and home. Read stories of the Magi and the Twelve Days of Christmas and sing Christmas carols. Light the Christ candle and pray.

Holy Light, shine on our world, open our hearts to be your light and carry your love into all we offer wherever we are …

BAPTISM OF THE LORD

… and the Holy Spirit descended upon him in bodily form like a dove. And a voice came from heaven, 'You are my Son, the Beloved; with you I am well pleased.'

Luke 3:22 (NRSV)

Baptised in water

In the beginning water,
born in water,
led through water,
baptised in water,
sealed by the Spirit.

Pouring out living water,
ebbing and flowing,
flooding and rising,
blessed and beloved,
named in baptism,
blessed by the Spirit.

Prayer moment

Historically, baptism has played a significant role in both Easter and Christmas seasons, from the birth narratives, to dying and rising with Christ. Find your baptismal certificate or a liturgy for baptism and set a bowl of water near you. Read through the words and touch the water. Remember, whether you are baptised or not, you are always a 'beloved child of God'. Thank God for loving you. As you touch the water, pray for ways to carry God's love out into the world.

Spirit of the living God, call me out of the waters of baptism, that I may use my gifts to care for your world …

PRESENTATION OF THE LORD/CANDLEMAS

Simeon took him in his arms and praised God, saying,
'Master, now you are dismissing your servant in peace,
* according to your word …'*

Luke 2:28–29 (NRSV)

In the temple

In the Temple,
the child's father and mother marvelled at what they heard.
Simeon said, 'a sword will pierce your soul',
and his words pierced the hearts of all.
He blessed them to lift the veil from their eyes.

Anna marvelled and gave thanks
because she too saw the promise,
the mystery of grace revealed
through Mary, Holy Mary, Mother of God,
bringing light into the world,
enough to deliver us,
enough to pierce the veils we hide behind.

Gift of God, unbroken thread,
a light that shines for all,
a light that shone from a tree,
blessing women, blessing men, blessing all.
Mary, Mother of God, sing your song of praise, again.

Prayer moment

Like crystals turning in a kaleidoscope, the liturgical focus for today varies, from Jesus' presentation in the Temple to the purification of Mary and the Feast of Candlemas marking forty days after Christmas. These are all images worthy of our reflection. Choose an icon or an image from art that reflects one of these times and focus on it. What attracts you or disturbs you? Continue to meditate with the image or icon until you feel God's presence.

Child of the Temple, holy is your name and blessed am I that your grace touches me and all of us, women and men; may your love carry us through our lives …

PRAYING OUR WAY FORWARD

Then I heard the voice of the Lord saying, 'Whom shall I send, and who will go for us?' And I said, 'Here am I; send me!'

Isaiah 6:8 (NRSV)

Open the door

Open the door, go ahead
walk through it,
nothing is stopping you but you.
So, go ahead,
open your heart to change.
Allow the past to bless you into the present,
take the best with you.
God was and is and will be forever.
Go ahead, open the door.

Do not stay in the past.
Do not carry it with you and miss the present;
you have enough to carry already.
Today's worries are enough for today.
What is done is done, be where you are.
Go ahead, open the door.

Prayer moment

Whatever the time of the year, there are always times of 'crossing over', of moving from one stage/one period of life to another. Reflect on the past year, and what your dreams are for the future. To help do this, you might draw a map of your life by marking significant moments (with words or figures) on a line leading to where you are today; then mark what you are wishing for in the future. Your map may curve around or be a straight line across the page. Then set your map aside and be still in your mind and body. Thank God for all those who have walked with you on your journey, and for those who will accompany you in the future. You could do this in a group too and have each person tell their story through sharing their map.

God of all seasons, I am crossing into new territory and I thank you for watching over me on all the roads of my life. You were with me through many Covid days and all other troubles I have seen, and now I need to know that you will walk with me again, as I find my way back and pray my way forward through all that is yet to be ...

Sources and acknowledgements

Passages from NRSV copyright 1989, Division of Christian Education of the National Council of the Churches of Christ in the United States of America. Used by permission. All rights reserved.

Some of the pieces in this book were first published in the download *Praying with Light: In Candlemas and Starless Nights*, by Rebeka Maples, Wild Goose Publications, 2017, and in *Spring: Liturgical Resources*, edited by Ruth Burgess, Wild Goose Publications, 2019.

Wild Goose Publications, the publishing house of the Iona Community established in the Celtic Christian tradition of Saint Columba, produces books, e-books, CDs and digital downloads on:

- holistic spirituality
- social justice
- political and peace issues
- healing
- innovative approaches to worship
- song in worship, including the work of the Wild Goose Resource Group
- material for meditation and reflection

Visit our website at
www.ionabooks.com
for details of all our products and online sales